KINDERGARTEN:
TATTLE-TALES, TOOLS, TACTICS, TRIUMPHS and TASTY TREATS for TEACHERS and PARENTS

Susan Case

A funny thing happened on the way to learning...

AWOC.COM Publishing
Denton, Texas

Dedication

This book is dedicated to my publisher, husband and best friend, Dan Case who persuaded, encouraged, and bribed me to write a book about my teaching experiences. It is also dedicated to my daughter, Sarah, who has taken me on the fabulous journey of motherhood and who motivated me to return to school and become a teacher.

A Special Note of Thanks

Thank you, Peggy Moss Fielding, for teaching and inspiring me to write. Your faith in me and editorial expertise helped me to realize dreams can become reality. I want to also thank my sister, Diane Atkinson, for her countless hours of editing and offering kind words of encouragement and suggestions.

AWOC.COM Publishing
P.O. Box 2819
Denton, TX 76202

©2011 by Susan Dulin Case
All Rights Reserved.

No part of this publication may be reproduced, stored in a retrieval system, or transmitted in any form or by any means, electronic, mechanical, recording or otherwise, without written permission, except in the case of brief quotations embodied in critical articles and reviews.

Manufactured in the United States of America

ISBN: 978-0-937660-96-6

Visit Susan's blog at kindergartenbasics.blogspot.com

Table of Contents

Chapter One Teacher Tattle Tales 5

Chapter Two Celebrate the Holidays—Celebrate Life 17

Chapter Three A Smooth Move to School 37

Chapter Four Reading—the Greatest Gift of All 47

Chapter Five Science—Survival Specials 71

Chapter Six Discipline—Combat Duty or Common Sense Tactics? 83

Chapter Seven The Special Education Experience 103

Chapter Eight Silly Sanity Lists 115

Chapter Nine Recipes for Fun Fridays 125

Chapter Ten It's a Wonderful World, After All 145

Chapter One
Teacher Tattle Tales

Show and Tell

My kindergarten class had "Show and Tell" on Fridays. This was exciting for the children. It gave them a chance to sparkle and it gave me a chance to sit down.

I told my class they could bring their pets if they followed one simple rule. Their mom or dad needed to call me first so we could make arrangements. In kindergarten, the fewer surprises, the better.

The rule applied for both students *and* parents. I learned this lesson when a parent literally threw two ferrets into the room causing children to scream and run—some toward the ferrets and others away from the ferrets. S*ome* pets need to be accompanied by an adult.

I let parents know that I could provide a cage, if required. Of course, insects could be brought to class in a jar with no parental accompaniment. A little more questionable were fish coming in jars of splashing water.

Little Cody, like many kindergarteners, had either not heard the rule or had chose to ignore it. He knew he could shine in the spotlight if he were to bring his pet to school. One Friday, unknown to his mother, Cody put his small parakeet into his backpack and rode in the car to school. It is a miracle the little bird was not squashed.

Upon entering the room, Cody promptly released the bird with a, "ta-dah!" The poor thing flittered about the room causing children to scream and parents to look up in astonishment.

A dad finally caught the bird. I put it in my empty tarantula container. We had Show and Tell earlier than usual that day.

I called Cody's mother who had no idea that her darling son had brought the $60 bird to school. She said, "I wondered why he didn't want me to look in his backpack this morning."

Cody's frazzled-looking mom came to retrieve the bird. She was going to carry it to the car and drive home. I insisted that she take the bird home in a container. I didn't feel that it was safe for her to drive with a bird flying loose in the car. What was she thinking?

Teacher Tip: Be specific about Show and Tell. Put your rules in the Parent Newsletter. Some kindergarten teachers have stopped having Show and Tell because of increased academic pressures. But I strongly recommend letting students shine and express themselves for these few enlightening moments. You could let the weekly Super Star bring a Show and Tell, or let a few students each Friday participate by order of the first letter of their name. They can look at the behavior chart, if arranged alphabetically, to see their turn is in the future.

Teacher Tale: The most unusual Show and Tell was related to me quietly by another kindergarten teacher. Curious Calvin snuck his teenage sister's personal hygiene item to school. He thought surely his all-knowing teacher could explain why he couldn't play with it. The shocked teacher could not respond for a minute. Finally, she told Calvin to take it back home and maybe his mother could explain. This was definitely beyond the limits of her required curriculum. Maybe Calvin's mother would start checking her child's backpack now. One could always hope.

The Escaped Tarantula

It's important to have live critters in the classroom for the kindergartners to enjoy. It helps connect learning to our environment and it teaches them responsibility. I always had a variety of creatures in my classroom, either visiting or living there for years. The children voted on names for the pets. Each pet was labeled to help teach reading. At one time or another, my room had fish, turtles, lizards including a large iguana, snakes, ant colony, crabs, slugs, hamsters, butterflies, a borrowed rabbit, visiting horse (outside) and a baby duckling. Did you know cute fuzzy ducklings grow quickly into messy, noisy ducks?

I even had a tarantula. The children named him Leggy. I'm not sure why I had a poisonous creature in my classroom. My husband thinks I attended too many science workshops. It was probably because another teacher gave it to me. I've always been a sucker for freebies.

The problem arose when someone forgot to fasten the lid securely on the tarantula's container. It may have been me.

Yes, Leggy escaped. I was worried sick and emailed the teachers on my hallway to be on the lookout. I could not find Leggy anywhere and finally went home. My husband suggested that we go back that night with a flashlight. Tarantulas are nocturnal and we could possibly find Leggy with no children running around screaming. It would be a secret among our grade level teachers. We were sure the custodian would be delighted to let me in for such a reason.

But I got sick and never made it back to school that night. I had to call for a substitute. I knew a substitute, Mrs. Chance, who told me she liked being in my classroom. I had her number memorized and didn't often share it with other teachers. I was honest with Mrs. Chance about Leggy being loose and asked if she still wanted to sub. I think my voice sounded hoarse and pleading. She agreed, much to my astonishment. She insisted that she was surviving the raising of her four children, two with special needs, and was not afraid of a little tarantula. *Good, at least she is aware of the situation and can be on the lookout for Leggy.*

I waited until school was out then called Mrs. Chance. She had found Leggy! The tarantula was under a broom which was behind my desk. Mrs. Chance was going to sweep while the children were in special areas when she saw Leggy. She became nervous and retrieved the kindergarten teacher across the hall. Without hesitation, Mrs. Wilkins agreed to help. She found a container and scooped Leggy inside then encouraged him back into his sealed home. Mrs. Wilkins had participated with me in numerous science workshops and was also an advocate of having pets in the classroom. I knew I could count on her.

The unfortunate part was that Mrs. Wilkins thought all the teachers knew that my tarantula had escaped, not just the teachers in our hallway. So she promptly sent out an email to all the staff, which included the principal, to reassure them that my tarantula was now safely back in its container. I was embarrassed. Relieved, but embarrassed.

I decided it was time to pass the tarantula on to another naïve teacher who was younger and eager to please his students. I warned him to make sure the lid was secure after feeding time. He was thrilled to have the pet. I was thrilled he now had the responsibility for a tarantula.

Teacher Tip: Never take a day off when you have an escaped tarantula. Did you know that an escaped hermit crab can live for at least ten days without being in its container? I promise this is true as told to me by another kindergarten teacher. I also know that some fish can live in an aquarium the entire summer without being fed. I always took my aquariums home during the summer so I could care for the fish. But I know teachers whose fish survived the summer months with no attention, specifically guppies.

By the way, guppies have amazing reproductive abilities. And, if you acquire a "free" iguana, just know that you will need to make weekly trips to the pet store for live crickets. And free snakes love live goldfish or tiny mice (which also require weekly trips to the pet store). It is a thrill to watch snakes eat critters if you are a kindergartner. Not so much of a thrill for an adult who doesn't eat much meat.

Joke: The substitute teacher takes the class out for recess. When they return inside, she realizes she is missing a child. The staff helps the frantic teacher look all over the campus, but to no avail. Finally, the principal said, "I'll call Toby's house. He lives nearby. Perhaps he walked home."

"Yes, Toby is here," the mother told the principal. "He said he had a prostitute teaching class today and that she didn't know nothin'."

The principal politely answered, "He had a *sub*-stitute teacher in his class today, I know her personally and I can assure you she is not a *pros*-titute. Her husband is my preacher."

Nap Time—Yes or No?

Let's not kid ourselves. A nap, or a short rest time, is helpful. Kindergarten used to be half day in many states or even non-existent. But with more and more mothers joining the work force, and increased academic pressure, the trend is now for kindergarten to be full day. This can be a very *long* day for five and six year old children, and for their teachers.

My husband often commented that my job was like planning a day-long birthday party for twenty-two five-year-olds Monday through Friday. Five and six year old children have very short attention spans. Of course, good teachers learn that hands-on short assignments work best. This takes much planning and preparation.

Most children entering kindergarten have been in daycare, Head Start, private pre-kindergarten or a Mother's Day Out program. But each year, there are still a few children who have never been separated from their mothers for much time. These children need rest time. In fact, all children and adults need a rest time. So after lunch and a school mandated ten-minute walk to increase exercise, my kindergartners enjoyed rest time.

When I started teaching kindergarten, nap mats were on the school list. This was later deemed unnecessary because of the cost and the time to get the mats out and to put them back. Folding a mat can become a battle with some uncoordinated, or unwilling, children. But it is important to be able to define a resting space for each child that is their own. I had the children bring a towel which was kept in their cubby. It is easier for a child to stay on their own towel and keep their hands and feet to themselves rather than just have a spot on the floor with no boundaries. I found it best to spread the children around the room.

I was amazed at how many children wanted to tickle each other. But a few fell asleep giving me ten minutes of glorious down time which I used to recoup, pray for patience, and put afternoon materials on their desks. I never, ever woke a sleeping child unless we were going outside for recess or the last bell rang. Children need rest and sleep, especially if they are sick, don't have parents with enough sense to put them to bed by 8:00, are adjusting to Daylight Savings Time, or have been trick-or-treating and are recovering from a sugar coma.

Some parents and staff argue that rest time should be eliminated due to the demands of academics, even in kindergarten. I say, "Let them be children while they have a chance." Which is code for, "Let teachers have ten minutes to recover before the afternoon work."

I know children need quiet time because I've actually seen them place beanbags over their ears when they are too stimulated. This is a huge clue that some peace and quiet is desperately needed.

No More Swings or Wooden Benches

I was a stay-at-home mom for years before I began my teaching career in my forties. I was surprised to learn that schools didn't have swings anymore. I guess some child was hurt and lawyers put the fear into the school districts.

One day, when we went to recess, we found that the very long wooden bench surrounding the playground area had been removed. There was no place for the teachers and children to sit. The teachers were disappointed. Some amazing conversations had taken place on that long wooden bench.

When we inquired in the office about the removal of the long wooden bench, we were told that a child had gotten a splinter. We were assured that the Parent Teacher Association (PTA) would have another fundraiser in the Spring. If there was any money left, iron benches would be purchased and cemented into the ground. In the meantime, teachers could stand during recess or bring their own lawn chairs. This left us wondering if this was an insinuation that the children would be better watched if we didn't have a bench, or that perhaps shorter recesses were desired by the principal.

I stood on the days I forgot to carry my lawn chair outside. Eventually, the children reminded me and were eager to help carry it.

I missed the long wooden bench as much as I missed swings. I had attended numerous workshops which stated that swinging was good for the body. I already knew it was good for the soul. I think that bench was good for my body *and* my soul.

Important conversations had happened on that long bench. We kindergarten teachers supported each other, gave advice, and exchanged academic ideas. If it works, share it! This was our unspoken survival motto. We also exchanged humorous tidbits which is absolutely necessary to maintain any shred of sanity when working with large numbers of small children.

I remember one day when I was enjoying being outside and sitting on the long bench, my plump student, Lizzy, joined me. She was struggling to read and had low self-esteem because of her weight. I learned from other teachers that her siblings had struggled in school also. Her father told me he didn't learn to read until third grade. He was now wearing a police uniform and enrolled in law school—another late bloomer. I could relate.

It was a hot day and Lizzy kept asking when recess would be over. Since it was Friday, we took twenty minutes instead of the allotted fifteen minutes. She needed every second of this time to exercise but my encouragement did nothing to budge her off the bench.

Finally, she put her glittering gold purse on her head and stuck her face into it. She was making an unspoken understatement. *I've had enough of school already today.* I could empathize. Some school days were too much for any person, struggling or not. But hiding her face inside her glittering purse made me laugh. Kindergarten children will say, or do, anything.

Many months later, our playground proudly displayed two iron benches. They were still located in the bright Texas sunshine, but we could at least sit down. The teachers passed around the sunscreen and continued their supportive humorous conversations.

Teacher Tip: Play is an expression of the soul. Take children to a park to swing. I still swing when the opportunity presents itself. It is very good for tightening the stomach muscles, plus it's just plain fun. Recently, my sister and I rode on a Merry-go-Round at a mall because my daughter encouraged us to join her. Spinning makes everyone smile.

Our school was fortunate to have a park within walking distance. We were allowed to take the children without a permission slip because our school paid for a sidewalk to the park. If you are not this fortunate, take a field trip to a park. You don't have to drive long distances for field trips. The thrill is in riding the bus, singing songs, and laying your head on a friend's shoulder for a nap on the way back to school.

Birthday Celebrations

My birthday went unnoticed by parents and students year after year. It was remembered by my grade level team and that was plenty for me. We ate together in the classroom and I was treated to lunch. Someone brought a chocolate cake or brownies. What could be better? But one year, all that changed.

I was reading a book to the children when several parents, and the principal, walked into my room. *Now what?* These were friendly parents, and it was my birthday, so I remained optimistic that I wasn't in trouble for anything.

"Surprise! You're getting a massage, facial, manicure and pedicure for your birthday!" proudly announced the room mom.

I'm sure I looked very surprised which wasn't helped when several children asked, without even raising their hands, "What's a massage?"

"It's fine," Mrs. Staniszewski, the principal, assured me with a sheepish grin on her face. "These parents are going to watch your class this afternoon while you get pampered. You'd better hurry. Your appointment is in fifteen minutes. Just go!"

I thanked them, grabbed my purse, and quickly walked in long strides out of the building. I couldn't be seen running because it was against the rules. I'd been treated to several massages over the years, but I'd never had a facial, pedicure, or manicure. Plus, I had the afternoon off for pampering myself! This was going to be a great birthday for my tired body.

I was in heaven as the masseuse rubbed my back releasing tension that had been building since summer. Then my face was scrubbed, a curious shade of green goo applied, and a hot towel placed on my tingling face. Afterward, I followed directions by breathing deeply while a divine moisturizer was applied and gently massaged into my desperately dry and wrinkling skin.

Next was the manicure and pedicure. I placed my feet in a hot whirlpool while the young manicurist, with jeweled decals on her nails, offered suggestions on my nail care. *Bless her heart.* She then offered even more suggestions on toenail care. However, I didn't feel too embarrassed, as I knew I probably would never see her again as this kind of pampering was rare for teachers.

The heavenly treatment was eventually over. I thought I'd better go back to the classroom even though I knew the students had been dismissed. I wanted to make sure I was prepared for the next day.

To my astonishment, the desks had been pushed to the side and rearranged, the centers (work or play stations) were mixed together, and there were no papers to be found for me to grade by drawing happy faces on them. It took me an hour to get everything back in order.

Did I forget to tell the parents what the children did in kindergarten? Couldn't they find the afternoon lesson plans and papers? The next day, my questions were answered. The room mom showed up saying, "My, you sure don't get paid nearly enough for your job. We pushed the desks away and let them dance and then couldn't seem to get them to sit back down and do any work. After a very long recess, we let them go to centers for the rest of the day. I've added you on my prayer list."

Maybe in my hurry to the appointment, I'd forgotten to explain the afternoon's work. Maybe I'd forgotten to show the parents where the work was located. Whatever the reason, I had a great afternoon of pampering and the students had an afternoon of fun. But I think we were all a little relieved for things to return to "normal." Even the mischievous students did their work and told me that they loved me.

Teacher Tip: Always make sure substitutes, and surprise parent babysitters, are clear about student work and leave it in a visible place on your desk. Make a room diagram in case desks and centers are rearranged while you are gone. This will save you time if you have to put the room back together. I'm sure you have a reason why little Susie sits by Sammy instead of talkative Sally.

Birthday Party Tips: Eat cupcakes outside. I've seen children squash them on their smiling face and proudly stick out a purple gooey tongue. Cupcakes are messy. The most fun my kindergartners had for a birthday celebration was when a grandmother brought huge homemade sugar cookies. The children decorated them with frosting, M&M's, gummy bears, chocolate chips and sprinkles. Some children made a face, or design, on the cookie using the candy. I think they had more fun decorating the cookies than eating them. I've included several good sugar cookie recipes in Chapter Nine.

Play is the highest expression of human development in childhood for it alone is the free expression of what is in the child's soul. ~Fredrich Froebel

Chapter Two
Celebrate the Holidays—Celebrate Life

Halloween—Spider Web Ceilings

It is becoming more common for schools to call Halloween a Fall Celebration in order not to offend any religious sect. If your school does not think it is politically, or spiritually, correct to celebrate Halloween, you might consider Character Day when staff and students dress as a character from a book. Whatever you call it, it can be a time to celebrate, fantasize, and role play.

Many schools do not allow children to wear costumes to school. Yes, costumes can be distracting. Some parents let their precious Darth Vader come to school with a fake weapon and a scary mask. Little princesses want to wear glittery Dorothy shoes and angels want to wear large wings. Parents send notes asking that the shoes and wings not be damaged during recess and Physical Education (PE). *Give me a break.*

Our school's solution was to have a Friday evening Fall Carnival/Fundraiser. Children could wear costumes leaving their masks and weapons at home. Parents could assure their children that they would have the opportunity to scare the neighbors later in full attire.

If Halloween fell on a school night, teachers knew their students would either be hyper from the sugar, or comatose. I've seen children coming off the morning school bus sucking on sugar sticks. Some proudly told me that their Halloween candy was their breakfast. *Gee, thank you parents.*

Call it Science

I always had a science theme in my classroom during October. We legitimately studied nocturnal animals such as bats, spiders, raccoons, moths, coyotes, foxes, and tarantulas. I bought fluffy spider webs and stretched them across the ceiling. The children made spiders by tracing a large and a small circle with chalk on black paper then fan-folded eight legs. This can be an interesting challenge for some. Children love squiggly eyes and they were encouraged to use lots of glue (a rarity) and patiently let the eyes dry, also challenging for some. They also traced bats on black paper. I hung the creatures from the ceiling using yarn and paperclips.

My class thought this was the most amazing ceiling. The children learned that spiders have eight legs and insects have only six. I learned that anything hanging from a ceiling enhances and lengthens the time kindergartners will rest during naptime.

Joke: What does a Texas ghost wear? BOOts!

Thanksgiving—Gratitude and Grace

You know you're a kindergarten teacher when you wake up humming "Any Turkey Can Tango." The kinder classes practiced this song with movements for weeks before the big finale of a feast and performance for the parents. You can watch children singing and dancing to this song on the Internet and even order the book and CD. Just Google the words *any turkey can tango*.

During the month of November, kindergarten children learn about the founding of our country, American Indians, Pilgrims and gratitude. The children in my classroom wanted to become American Indians for the special feast day while other kinder students became pilgrims or turkeys.

My room moms cut paper sacks to make fringed vests for the children to sponge paint. The children loved painting them with die-cut sponges of turkeys, moon shapes, stars, and leaves. Volunteers cut feathers from colored paper for headbands. At the end of every day, a child was rewarded with a feather if they stayed on green—the desired color on my behavior chart.

During the week before Thanksgiving, it became very obvious who had good behavior by simply looking at the number of feathers on a child's headband. Children blossomed into perfection, or at least tried harder to stay on green. Sure, many feathers and headbands were lost and broken. But it was worth repairing headbands and replacing feathers for the improved behavior.

Some children wanted a pattern of colored feathers, some wanted all the same color, and some were just plain desperate for any color. Feather earning is a useful reward—or a legitimate threat.

Placemats woven by the children are a lofty goal but can be accomplished with the help of volunteers. The strips should already be glued on one side before the children start weaving. Weaving two colors is a wonderful way for the children to have a hands-on experience with a simple pattern. But weaving can be very difficult for some children. If I did not have enough adults to help, I let children who were finished with their placemat help other students. Gratefulness is a welcome sight at any age.

The children made invitations to the feast which were included in the weekly Monday Folder. Parents and grandparents were invited with a suggested food contribution. I taped butcher paper on the students' tables for them to color. They traced their hands making turkeys, colored patterns, drew shapes, and wrote "I love you, Mom" or whatever creative notion they desired. They also practiced printing the theme words. I also kept a large chart visible with holiday words for the children to learn. I drew a picture clue beside the words. The children told me what words were important to them. By the end of the theme, many children were able to read all the words and some were using them in sentences.

Finally, the Thanksgiving feast day arrived. Children proudly entered the classroom carrying food. They wore their headbands and vests as we practiced "Any Turkey Can Tango" one more time. Lunchtime approached as parents eagerly came to school with some pushing baby strollers. They formed a line with their precious child for a plate of food. We had volunteers put food on the plates so that the last in line would have a chance to eat a sample of everything. Finally, we all sat down to eat. Teachers asked each child what they were thankful for and received answers like, "My family." "My dog." "My T-ball team." "My Wii."

Finally, we waited for the last child to answer. The sweet little girl said, "I'm thankful for God and for baby Jesus."

I said, "Amen to that. Let's eat."

Then a boy said, "Aren't we going to say grace?"

I proudly responded, "Yes, we are. Who would like to say a blessing on the food?"

No child volunteered but a parent answered, "I'd like to say it."

This may have been the first blessing some children heard on food but it was the best grace I've ever heard. We bowed our heads as this returned soldier thanked God for the freedoms enjoyed our country and for our soldiers placed in harm's way. He thanked God for our country's leaders, food, friends, and teachers. I felt very blessed to be included in this hero's prayer.

After the feast was finished, all the kindergartners were lead outside and they formed a large circle. They performed "Any Turkey Can Tango" complete with loud singing and choreographed dancing. This grand performance brought a smile to every face.

Teacher Tip: Stone Soup is a wonderful book to read during Thanksgiving time but I do not recommend having soup for your feast. One year we tried to make soup from ingredients students donated. This can be very messy if the entire grade level of kindergartners are gathered together to eat on the floor. Invariably, some children will need to use the restroom. Children accidentally, but easily, kick over bowls on the floor. The kindergarten teachers agreed to have finger foods for future feasts.

Marcia Brown wrote *Stone Soup* in 1947. According to the story, some travelers came to a village, carrying nothing more than an empty pot. Upon their arrival, the villagers are unwilling to share any of their food with the hungry travelers. The travelers filled the pot with water, dropped a large stone in it, and placed it over a fire in the village square. One of the villagers became curious and asked what they are doing. The travelers answered that they were making stone soup which tastes wonderful, although it still needs a little bit of garnish to improve the flavor. The villager doesn't mind parting with just a little bit of flour to help them out. Other curious villagers walked by and little by little ingredients are added. Finally, a delicious and nourishing pot of soup is enjoyed by all.

Another story exists about stone soup. In the United States, during the Great Depression, families were unable to put food on the table every day. It became a practice to place a large and porous rock in the bottom of the stock pot. On days when there was food, the stone would absorb some of the flavor. On days when there was no food, the stone was boiled, and the flavor would come out of the stone into the water, producing a weak soup, which was better than not eating.

Teacher Tip: Check your clothes before you go to the store after a day of sponge painting. I was at the grocery store wearing my teacher sweater when a lady approached me and said, "You must be a teacher. Do you know you have a leaf sponge attached to your sweater?" The sweater and holiday jewelry probably gave her a clue—but the attached sponge was the clincher.

We both laughed and I said, "It's better than having a *Kick Me* or *Kiss Me* note attached."

Christmas—The Funny Smelling Perfume

After hurricane Katrina hit, our Texas town had numerous evacuees from the Gulf Coast, some who stayed. One such student was named Marcus. He was a quiet and humble boy, behind academically, poorly dressed, but respectful.

His mother wanted him to do well in school. She supported me whenever I had a suggestion. It was obvious that she cared deeply for her son and respected teachers. I'm sure she never had the opportunity to attend college. But she was strong enough that a hurricane wasn't going to ruin her life or that of her son. I felt inspired by her to become a better teacher.

Christmas was approaching and I asked the children what they wanted Santa Claus to bring them. This was intended as a learning tool. They were to draw a picture and write about it. Their third grade Reading Buddies would help them write the words when they came in on Friday afternoon. I promised the children that I would send their letter to Santa home and their parents would know where to mail it. It would be delivered to the North Pole from the post office.

The children and I were sitting in a circle on the floor. It was Marcus' turn to answer the question.

"I would like a bike. I left mine in New Orleans and we're never going back there."

I had to fight back tears. I knew they had brought nothing from New Orleans, not even family. They had been living at a camp until other arrangements could be made.

After school, I sent out an email to see if anyone had an extra bike. A teacher responded that she would bring her child's old bike. The next day she brought several bikes. They weren't in the best condition but they were fixable. I called Marcus' mother and ask her if she would like to come pick up the bikes. Or, if she preferred, when my husband got back into town, he could repair the bikes. She said, "I'm on my way."

I met her in the parking lot with her boyfriend who had recently arrived from New Orleans. Their smiles were huge when they saw the bikes. Her boyfriend shook my hand in his large hands and thanked me. He assured me that he would fix the bikes, paint them, and find a home for the extra bikes. I knew he would.

At Christmas time, Marcus proudly brought me a gift in a zip-lock baggie. It was powder and perfume. It smelled a little funny to me but I like it. I still remember how proud Marcus was to give it to me. Occasionally I smell it and put some on. I don't remember who gave me some of my other gifts, most of which were more expensive, and all of which were wrapped nicer.

Teacher Tip: Give what you can, let others help you when you can't do it all, and give older children a chance to serve. Our school has third grade Reading Buddies for the kindergartners. On Friday afternoons, a third grade class visits a kindergarten class and reads the child's library book. This gives the teacher a little relief, helps the children appreciate their library books more, and builds a relationship with an older student whom, one hopes, will encourage a love of reading.

Teacher, Do You Believe in Santa Claus?

Much of teaching in kindergarten is reading books, asking questions, encouraging/deciphering answers, and writing words on a white board to foster the reading/writing connection. A child will ask this question every year in December, "Teacher, do you believe in Santa Claus? My cousin said he's not real!"

"Yes, I do believe in Santa Clause. He visits my house because I try to be a good person."

I was not allowed to initiate a conversation about God in the classroom. But if a child asked, I could answer. And I did. I answered, "I believe in God and in His son, Jesus Christ. Jesus is my friend and helps me know right from wrong. I feel better when I do what is right." To my knowledge, no parent ever complained about my saying these words.

Christmas

During the month of December, put seasonal cookie cutters in the art center for tracing along with colored pencils. Ask the children to cut out their traced ornaments for the tree. I was blessed with a small tree given to me by the teacher who previously enjoyed the classroom. She intended to throw it away because the lights no longer worked, but I rescued it and wrapped even more lights around it. This poor old tree was proudly displayed for many years with an astonishing assortment of homemade paper ornaments. I also hung lights across the room from the ceiling. This too can increase rest time and gives a magical tone to the room especially while playing Enya or Andrea Bocelli CDs.

During the Christmas season, encourage children to draw a picture to be taken to a nursing home. Maybe their third grade Reading Buddy could help them with a note such as "Merry Christmas. I love you." This may be the only gift some residents receive. Also, you can send cards and drawings to soldiers through the

American Red Cross *Holiday Mail for Heroes* campaign. Visit the web www.redcross.org. This program collects holiday cards and delivers them to wounded warriors, deployed service members, military families and veterans. Do not send them to Walter Reed Army Medical Center because they must be screened by volunteers before being delivered.

Let the school counselor know of children whose families may not be able to afford Christmas presents or food for the holidays. Some parents, or your church, may be eager to help with gently used toys, books, clothes and food. There is a growing trend to help within one's own community. Sometimes it is just a matter of communication and services are provided.

In December, I always wrote in my newsletter that the children would love to have new crayons, markers, pencils and bottles of glue in their Christmas stocking. Something as simple as a new box of crayons can make a child's face beam. I also let parents know that donations to the classroom would be greatly appreciated. Face reality, one bottle of glue and one box of crayons will not last through the school year.

The Christmas Party (aka The Winter Party)

Our school invited parents to a musical performance of several grade levels. Afterwards, each classroom had a holiday party. In my newsletter, I asked parents to send a wrapped new, or gently used, "Golden Book" with no name on it to put under the tree. The kindergarten teachers always had extra wrapped books for those children who didn't bring one. I collected them at garage sales. Often they were given to me for free when I explained why I wanted them.

The book exchange is a version of "musical chairs."Arrange the books in a circle. Play music as the children walk around the outside of the books. When the music stops, let the children pick up a book in front of them for their present. At first, I didn't let children exchange their book with someone else thinking it would be too chaotic. But I eventually gave in, emphasizing that no one needed to trade their book if they wanted to keep it.

It is great fun for the children to play games blindfolded, such as "Pin the Nose on Rudolph." I had a poster board with a deer drawn on it and enough red circles for everyone to have a "nose." Beforehand, prepare the children by explaining that the game is just for fun. I was shocked the first time a child cried over this simple game. Some children have never played "Pin the Tail on the Donkey" and become very sensitive if others laugh, even while playing an innocent game. But children need to learn how to socialize, play games and be good sports.

I asked parents to make a contribution of food for our party. I found it best to give inexpensive items to those who couldn't afford to bring much such as bananas. If I thought a child could not, or would not, bring anything, I told them that we would have plenty of food and not to worry about it. I let parents know that extra food was appreciated and we always had plenty.

My Favorite Christmas Quote

*This
Christmas
mend a quarrel.
Seek out a forgotten
friend. Dismiss suspicion and
replace it with trust. Write a letter.
Give a soft answer. Encourage youth.
Manifest your loyalty in word and deed. Keep
a promise. Forgo a grudge. Forgive an enemy.
Apologize. Try to understand. Examine your demands
on others. Think first of someone else. Be kind. Be
gentle. Laugh a little more. Express your gratitude.
Welcome a stranger. Gladden the heart of a child.
Take pleasure in the beauty and wonder of the
earth. Speak your
love and then
speak it again.*
~Howard W. Hunter

I frame this quote for gifts using red and green Popsicle sticks or tongue depressors as an inexpensive frame. Thank goodness for the glue gun. Or I print the quote on pretty paper and stamp it with Christmas stamps. While the ink is wet, I sprinkle it with ultra fine Poly Flake Glitter which is so tiny it sticks to the ink. Everyone seems to appreciate the quote especially if accompanied by a small loaf of Pumpkin Bread or Strawberry Nut Bread. Recipes are included in Chapter Nine.

Joke: A teacher asked a student what he was drawing. "I'm drawing God," he replied.
"But, Johnny, nobody knows what God looks like."
He smiled and said, "You will when I'm finished."

All I Want for Christmas Is Your Two Front Teeth

Children are incredibly hard to understand as they lose their teeth and you lose your hearing, especially when you are outnumbered twenty-two to one.

During the month of December, we practiced songs and movements for the school holiday program as encouraged by the music teacher. After much movement and singing, I asked the children to sit on the floor while I read a book. I took off my shoes because my feet hurt.

A student named Dakota asked me, "Is your nose cold?"

I replied, "Oh, maybe my nose is a little cold."

"No," Dakota continued. "Is your toes cold?"

"Yes, my toes are cold." There, I hoped that satisfied her.

"I said 'are your toes gold?'" she persisted.

I looked down at my poorly manicured toenails which were indeed painted gold for the holiday season. *Will this child's permanent two front teeth ever be replaced? If not this year, hopefully her first grade teacher will receive that blessing.*

I had heard teaching first or second grades were much easier than teaching kindergarten. It had to be true. But there were never any openings in first or second grade at my school. Finally, there was an opening in second grade. I contemplated applying for it but then wondered if the older children loved their teacher unconditionally as mine did. Did they admire even the smallest of craft feats? Did they have centers, or group play/learning stations, to give the teacher somewhat of a break? I think not. I just stayed in kindergarten because my classroom was located in an older part of the building and had windows. The first and second grade classrooms were not that fortunate. I could see squirrels running up and down the trees, birds flying, and the weather. I knew when it snowed—a true rarity in Texas and a time to celebrate.

Joke: Whose idea was it to put an *s* in the word *lisp*?

Teacher Tip: Always let your students outside when it snows, especially if you live in a southern state. The snow may disappear before recess, or the last bell, and you will be sorry. Snow is science and PE and will prompt creative writing and art activities. It may not be in your lesson plans but it is a time to explore with the five senses. Scoop up some snow and make snowballs to put in the freezer. In the Spring, you can teach about the stages of water and remember that fun snowy day you shared.

Valentine's Day

Children love to celebrate anything and special days can easily be incorporated into lesson plans complying with your state's mandated curriculum. Valentine's Day is no exception.

Have the children trace hearts and cut them out making inexpensive Valentine's cards. They can draw pictures and print "I love you". Take the cards to a nursing home or send them to soldiers. Remember to keep updating your word chart with theme words they are interested in using and printing.

Ask a parent to die-cut numerous sizes of hearts from pink, red and purple paper. Encourage the children to glue the hearts making a transformer, action figure, animal, flower, insect, or whatever they like. Their third grade Reading Buddies could help them write about their creative art work.

The children can also use the die-cut hearts to glue on their Valentine's sack. You may need to help them print their name plainly on the top of the sack. I found it interesting that many kindergartners do not know the top from the bottom of a sack. Some children needed me to make dots forming the letters of their name for them to connect or I lightly printed their name and had them trace it in crayon.

Give the parents plenty of notice in your newsletter that their child needs to bring a Valentine for each student. Send home a class list of first names for the children to print on their Valentine's cards. I needed to encourage parents to help their child write the names on cards. Yes, it takes time, but children crave parental time especially if compliments and praise are lavishly given. It does not have to be perfect.

Place the children's decorated Valentine's sacks in alphabetical order by first name. Let the parents know that cards can be brought the entire week before the party. It helps the teacher to have cards put in sacks each day rather than all the students trying to do it the same day. Many children will need help but it is a great exercise in matching and reading. I let the higher level students help those who weren't reading yet.

Every year, some children come to school the day of the party with a box of cards and no preparation. Or some children come with no cards. I always had a few extra boxes for those children. You can buy them discounted after the holiday.

Ask a parent to make heart shaped cookies for the Valentine's party. In Chapter Nine, I've included my mother's prized Christmas sugar cookie recipe. It tastes wonderful and works well when you want to use cookie cutters. She never gave it out when she was alive but I now do it in her honor. It makes the best cookie I've ever tasted perhaps because it brings back so many childhood memories. However, her recipe does call for pecans so I've included several other sugar cookie recipes Chapter Nine.

Easter

Who doesn't love bunnies? I was fortunate to have a friend who let her son's pet rabbit visit our classroom. I let the children take turns sticking carrots and lettuce into the cage. The children loved having a soft furry animal visit and learned a lot about rabbits from books I read. The rabbit only visited one day but a first grade teacher had a beautiful pet rabbit which stayed in her classroom during the week and was taken home on the weekends by the Super Star. She let the rabbit out to hop around as a reward for good behavior. It was trained to potty in a litter box.

Let's have some fun amidst all the paperwork and academic pressure. Children love animals and movement. Practice the Bunny Hop. The music or PE teacher will teach it and you can reinforce the words and movements when the children need some action time. Call it PE, math or reading patterning, or just pure fun.

Last I knew, it was still all right to celebrate Easter at school. We always had an egg hunt and asked each child to bring a dozen plastic eggs filled with candy inside. I recommend that you let parents know the children should not bring plastic grass in their basket. It is difficult for the custodian to vacuum. Also, we learned it is too hot in Texas for chocolate candy which melts if the parents put it out too early. It is a good idea to have plenty of water available for those hot afternoon hunts.

Mother's Day, Madeline, and Great-Grandma

One memorable year, I had a precious girl named Madeline in my class. Her great-grandmother introduced herself to me on Meet the Teacher night. She told me she was raising Madeline because her granddaughter was in jail on drug related charges.

Madeline's great-grandfather also came to meet me while pulling his breathing machine. I was honored to meet them but wondered how long they would be able to take care of their bubbling bouncy five-year-old great-granddaughter.

Madeline had never been to any kind of school. She was anxious about being separated from her great-grandmother. She cried every day when she entered the room. It was heartbreaking. Some days, she cried during rest time. She'd been brave all morning and wanted to go home. Half-day kindergarten was no more but would have benefited this child. I tried to encourage Madeline. She was behind the other students but I knew she was a bright child.

Madeline gradually, but consistently, progressed academically, emotionally, and socially. After six weeks she didn't cry very often. By May, she was not crying at all, had finally adjusted, and was even reading on a lower level. Mother's Day was approaching and the children were busy making gifts to put in a personally decorated sack for their mother. They filled baby food jars with scented bath salts and glued colorful tissue paper squares on the jars. They drew pictures of what they loved doing with their mothers (very enlightening) and wrote love notes.

One of the kindergarten teachers thought we should have a Mother's Day Breakfast at 7:15 am with soft music, punch, and homemade muffins. I had learned a long time ago that teaching is about everyone else, certainly not about me (a survival tactic). I agreed that my class would also participate. I covered the children's desks with pink butcher paper. The children drew beautiful pictures of their mothers and wrote, "I love you, Mom."

I spent hours making colorful tissue corsages for the mothers. I froze a fruit ring to put in my pink punch bowl and made pumpkin bread (see Chapter Nine for the recipe). My husband bought grapes, bananas, and a huge bag of small donuts. Mothers offered to help but this was not allowed on *their* special day. When the famous morning approached, I was glad I had kept my daughter's little red wagon as I pulled my van close to the door to unload ice and food.

I was exhausted but knew the end of the year was approaching. Surely, I could manage one more special event. After all, who deserves pampering more than the mother of a kindergartner (other than their teacher)?

Freshly cut roses from my bushes adorned each table. The perfect Celtic CD played relaxing music which brought tears to tired mothers' eyes. I sprayed perfume in the air hoping no one was allergic to the flowers or the perfume.

Everything was going beautifully. Mothers were softly crying at their children's sweet notes, or berating siblings for helping themselves to yet another donut. I was feeling rewarded by giving moms a chance to be honored. I felt blessed because I know that giving is better than receiving.

Madeline arrived with her great-grandmother and two other women. I was introduced to Madeline's mother (who apparently had gotten out of jail) and to her neighbor (who soon told me that she loved Madeline and wanted to adopt her). I excused myself and went to the back of the room, pulled the tissue paper from the cabinet, and quickly made two more corsages.

All went well. No one fought over Madeline at the breakfast. The mothers rushed off to work with tears of appreciation and gratitude in their eyes, clutching their little sacks filled with notes and handmade gifts.

The great-grandmother told me that they would be moving to a cheaper apartment. They could not afford to live in their apartment and take care of Madeline too. I was told that Madeline would be going to another school next year. I never saw them after that school year although I often wondered and worried about their extended family.

Teacher Tip: Always make extra corsages. You never know who might attend.

Parent Tip: Don't do drugs or anything else that will jeopardize your ability to spend time with your child. You will miss many important events. You might have childless neighbors who want your precious job of parenting. You will leave children who are confused, angry or hurt, and teachers who are left wondering whatever happened to that sweet child. Try to have consistency and stability in your child's life with as few moves, and major changes, as possible. It's a well-known fact that secure children achieve to a much higher potential.

Field Day—Let There Be Winners

My husband and I sometimes do not agree. But on one thing we do agree: Let There Be Winners!

Everyone *can* become a winner at something. Talents can be found in all children. My special needs' daughter won first place in her category in the school's art contest. Her work was displayed at the district level and she won a first place medal in that category. She did not win the relay race on Field Day, but she was recognized in another area.

Competition is good because it prepares you for adulthood. Having everyone receive an equal award diminishes the true winner of an event and relaxes the incentive to win. Everyone can earn a Participatory Ribbon. But winners deserve special recognition in their event. Let hard workers and gifted athletics shine on Field Day.

When was anything really worthwhile easy? ~Richard G. Scott

Splash Day—Teach About Water

Let's be honest. The children aren't listening or learning the last week of school. They know summer is near and you won't be their" boss" anymore. Some are ecstatic, some are sad, and some don't know how to feel. Splash Day is something to hang over their heads for good behavior during the last desperate week when everyone is exhausted.

Some Do's

- Do Splash Day—which is defined as letting the children wear bathing suits while they play in water. Let them enjoy being kids and have good memories of school. They will be more likely to want to come back in the Fall.
- Do ask for parent volunteers, especially fathers.
- Do have parents send towels and sunscreen along with a permission note to apply sunscreen.
- Do save plastic spray bottles throughout the year.
- Do wear clothes that you don't mind getting wet. Wear flip-flops (which are not called *thongs* anymore like when I was growing up in Kansas).
- Do bring a change of clothes in case you need them.
- Do put hoses together and fill wading pools *away* from the building. This will allow for some of the mud and grass to disappear before entering the building.
- Do ask for parent volunteers to fill water balloons.
- Do encourage the children to pick up what's left of the balloons so that animals don't choke on the plastic.

Some Don'ts

- Don't let children change clothes unattended. Let one gender at a time change clothes in the room. This is where the father volunteers are needed. It is not a good idea to open the classroom door to naked little boys running around even though you've given them plenty of time to change into dry clothes. Some have a problem taking off wet clothes and putting dry clothes on a wet body.
- Don't forget to apply sunscreen to your own exposed parts. Bring a hat, sunglasses and lawn chairs. You won't have a chance to sit down, but somebody's grandmother might need a chair.
- Don't let the kids spray you if you are susceptible to catching pneumonia. Sometimes wet hair and air conditioning can lead to a cold or infection.
- Don't let the children blow bubbles on top of cement. It becomes slippery.
- Don't make promises to parents that you won't be able to keep, such as: "Your wading pool will be returned intact." "Your slippery slide will remain undamaged." "All swimming toys will be returned to their rightful owner."

Joke: "Do you know what it means when we say the weather is hot and humid?"

The kindergartner promptly answered, "Yea, it means it's too hot for humans."

Chapter Three
A Smooth Move to School

What do you remember about kindergarten? I remember my nap rug. I was proud of my pink chenille throw rug and it was my life blanket. I remember swinging and climbing during recess. I remember many goulashes stacked against the wall under our coats. We had Indian Chief Tablets and crayons. Life was simpler back then and much less stressful in a slow-paced small Kansas town.

This chapter is dedicated to parents who are willing and eager to help their child prepare for school. There are many opportunities for parents to help their child's readiness and reduce the amount of stress experienced by children and parents.

Children are excited about starting school, yet also a little afraid. Starting school means changes in their daily routine including being away from home, learning new rules, and following directions from other adults.

It's natural to have doubts and fears about change. Talk to your child about what they can expect. This will help you both feel more secure. Make sure your child's immunizations are up-to-date and keep a record to bring to school. Schools also ask for proof of residence such as a utility bill.

Practice healthy habits, including having children wash their hands before eating and after using the bathroom. Children need to take regular baths or showers and brush their teeth at least twice a day. Encourage your child to dress him or herself. Teach your child how to use zippers and buttons. Let them put their shoes on and take them off. Some children are able to tie their shoes before entering school. This takes lots of practice, persistence and praise. If they haven't mastered tying their shoes, don't worry about it and continue to practice when the child is interested. They will become more interested as they watch other children tie shoes.

It is disheartening for a teacher when a tired child enters the classroom at 8:00 a.m. saying, "I'm hungry. When are we going to eat?" A good night's sleep and a healthy breakfast are necessities for a happy productive morning.

At least two weeks before school starts, adjust your child's sleeping and eating times with the school's schedule. Children entering kindergarten should be in bed by 8:00 p.m. Young children need ten to twelve hours of sleep each night. Limit television time to no more than one or two hours a day. Encourage your child to play outside at least an hour a day. They need vitamin D (good old fashion sunshine) for strong bones and teeth.

Before your child starts kindergarten, walk or drive by the school. Perhaps you can play on the playground when school is not in attendance. Show your child how he or she will get to school and where you will meet afterwards. You, or a trusted adult, should always go with your child to a bus stop and be there at the end of the school day. Most schools will not permit the younger grades to be dismissed without an adult waiting.

Good Manners and Choices

Say "please" and "thank you" often and your child will too. Explain that good manners help people get along with each other and make friends. Teach your child how to listen without interrupting.

Explain why sharing toys with others is important. Sharing helps everyone have more fun. Play a card or board game that involves taking turns. Explain that games are for learning, as well as for fun. Demonstrate good sportsmanship. Ask children to pick up toys at the end of play. Thank them for helping. Praise your child often when you see him sharing toys, cleaning, or helping others. Help your children use words, not force, when they are angry. Use words to talk about feelings such as happy, sad, excited, worried, scared, curious or hurt. Communicate your thoughts and feelings to your child and have conversations. Explain that children are expected to raise their hand when they want to ask the teacher a question at school.

Let your child make choices between two good choices, such as what clothing to wear, book to read, or game to play. Let your child help make decisions about what to wear to school following the school's clothing policies. Choose clothes that are comfortable and easy for toileting. Tennis shoes are highly recommended due to recess and PE. Making choices builds independence and self-confidence forming an *I can do it* attitude. Compliment children on the skills they have already accomplished. Encourage them to make morally right decisions.

Play

Promote the artist in your child. If possible, provide crayons, large sheets of paper, safety scissors, play dough, sidewalk chalk, washable paint and markers. Use lavish praise to build confidence and skills with this creativity time. Buy puzzles, books, art supplies and games inexpensively at garage sales. Let the seller know you would appreciate whatever does not sell. Perhaps the seller will give it to you at a discount price or even free for saving him the trouble of disposal. Gently used books are often sold for huge discounts or given away.

Help your child learn the names of basic colors. The primary colors are red, yellow and blue. All colors are made from these three. At the dollar store, buy water colors and mix the paints to make purple, green, orange, pink and gray.

Help your child learn the basic shapes of square, triangle, circle and rectangle. Count objects to 10 and teach number recognition 1 through 5. Sort things by color, size, texture, or purpose.

Make learning fun. For example, "Is there something blue in this room?" Give your child a notebook and play Blue's Clues. Help your child find different shapes in the environment. Compliment them for being a good detective.

Play music and dance with your child or march together. Teach your child to catch, throw and kick a ball. Play "follow the leader." Have your child copy everything you do when you hop, skip, jump and clap. Let your child lead you with their ideas or patterns. Performing simple patterns enhances reading and math skills as does singing chants that rhyme while jumping rope.

Give your child simple tasks that involve matching, sorting or counting objects. Any interesting objects will work such as marbles, cards, M&M's, cereal, pasta, coins, shells, beans, yarn, buttons, socks, towels and utensils. Help them make a collection of rocks, bugs, stamps, coins, balls, leaves or anything that interests them.

Communicate

Decode your child's questions. A curious child's questions may seem never ending but they reflect a child's cognitive and emotional development. Parents should take their child's questions seriously and answer in a way that will strengthen and deepen the relationship. Don't always say "yes." Say yes only when it is in the child's best interest. Be objective and help children take responsibility for their behavior.

Talk to your child as you do chores. Questions that begin with *who, what, when, where* or *why* can encourage your child to talk and think. Help your child develop thinking skills such as being able to pay attention and follow simple instructions. Gradually, increase the steps in following instructions.

Teach your child to say their first and last name, clearly and loudly. The cafeteria worker needs a child's first and last name when they purchase a meal. Help your child memorize their address and phone number.

Have your child make friends with neighborhood children who will be entering school. Swap babysitting time. Mother's Day Out programs, church attendance and community preschool activities offer opportunities for children to learn social interaction skills. Preschool or pre-kindergarten classes help prepare children for kindergarten but never underestimate the time a mother and child spend together.

Teach your children to print their names with only the first letter capitalized. They can trace their name over and over in different colors. This is called *rainbow coloring*. Put dots on paper to form their name. Then they can connect the dots forming the most precious word in their universe—their first name. Help them form the letters of their name using M&Ms, beans, or marbles and let them run their fingers over the objects.

Tell your child about the fun things you did when you were in school such as art, music, games, centers and recess. Stay positive about school and be proud of your child for going to school. Encourage your child to always ask questions and share feelings with you.

Parents can contribute greatly to the adjustment of their child to school. But remember that it may take six weeks for a child to adjust to kindergarten. I've noticed surprised parents when I tell them how wonderfully behaved their child is at school. They tell me their kindergartner "lets off steam" after school and acts out.

I think this is normal after a long day of trying to please adults. They are tired and need rest and pampering too.

Supplies

Attend Spring Kindergarten Round-Up and Fall Meet the Teacher Night. Find out what school supplies your child will need and have them ready for that first day. Most schools have parent/teacher associations such as The Parent Teacher Association (PTA) who offer a school pack. It is a convenient way to buy your child's recommended supply list. However, discount stores offer school supplies at huge markdowns during the summer months. The stores often have your child's school supply list. Ask someone if you cannot find it. The supply list may also be available on the school's web site.

It is a good idea to purchase numerous supplies at the discounted price and save them for later in the year, especially crayons, glue and markers. These make great stocking stuffers. Kindergartners are thrilled with a new box of crayons or markers. It is much cheaper to buy them during the summer sales.

Perhaps you can afford to purchase some school supplies for a child in need. It is a sad sight for a scared five-year-old to come to school with no supplies. You can brighten a child's day by having extra supplies and a crayon box available. Your child's kindergarten teacher will be extremely grateful, as well. (I'm just thankful that I retired before toilet paper was on the list).

Family Time

Cultivate family time. Meet once a week for a family meeting. Eat dinner together and ask your children about their day. Make a conscious commitment to the priorities of marriage and family. Reinvent time management with an emphasis on your family. Make communication your constant goal. Create identity, security and motivation for children through family traditions and responsibilities. Emphasize values and morals in which the focus shifts away from wrong to the rewards and fulfillment of doing what is right. In other words, be there for your child. Children don't care about "quality time," they just want "time."

Stay-at-Home Moms—A Dying Bred

The first five years of a child's life are the most important for bonding, developing security, building self-esteem, fostering morality, and learning. These years are crucial and are a great predictor of how far a person will reach their potential, how happy they will become, and how much they will contribute to society. If you are a stay-at-home mother, consider it a blessing for you and your children to have this precious time together.

On the other hand, it is now becoming more common for parents to "red-shirt" their five-year old. This is a sport's term and refers to holding a child back a year before entering the school system. Some states do not mandate kindergarten. According to research, first-graders who don't go to kindergarten are typically behind their peers in their academic and social development, and are more likely to flunk a grade in elementary school. The trouble is, making kindergarten mandatory costs money.

Although kindergarten is not mandatory in all states, federal funding is partially provided in all states. The statistics vary on how many states mandate kindergarten. These figures give an approximate view as the numbers change yearly. Half day classes are required in 12 states, 12 states require full day, while 26 states offer a combination of both programs, leaving the decision to the local school districts.

Children who attend preschool, Headstart, and even kindergarten may be better prepared for first grade.

However, the benefits begin to fade out around second or third grade. By fifth grade, there is no proven advantage from those who did not attend any school before first grade.

One of the most widespread sources of childhood stress is the separation of a child from their parents at young ages. Declining parental attachment is an extremely serious risk to children today. The verdict of enormous psychological literature is that time spent with a parent is the very clearest correlate of healthy child development. Some research indicates it is advisable to move away from formal academic instruction to a developmental approach for early childhood education. With dedicated parents, children who are at home until first grade, can develop the skills necessary for learning and thus be prepared for an academic setting. Parents should be allowed to make the decision about their child attending kindergarten. Parents know their children better than anyone else.

Maturity

Dr. Jean Piaget, long respected in the academic community for his studies in human developmental research, found a child's cognitive abilities usually show maturity between the ages of seven and nine. Some children are put at risk by compulsory attendance statutes that do not take into account slower maturation rates. This is especially true with boys, and even more so if they have a summer birthday

In the state of Texas, kindergarten is not mandatory. A five year old may be allowed to wait to attend kindergarten the following year, rather than be enrolled in first grade, if the parents think this is best for their child. A six year old child can be tested and then a determination made if the child should be enrolled in kindergarten or in first grade, if a parent requests the testing.

I taught the last ½ day kindergarten class in my district. The demand had dwindled so that only one afternoon class was offered for the entire district. (I taught special education students in the morning, thus making me a full-time teacher.) Due to the increase in working mothers, ½ day kindergarten is no longer in demand enough to justify a full-time teacher in most districts. As the government increases the number of school days, parents have lower costs of daycare. But beware of the family and societal consequences.

You and your child are very fortunate indeed if you are a stay-at-home parent. Many communities offer support/play/learning groups for preschoolers. Due to our current economy, the job market, and greater opportunities to work from home, the trend is reversing and mothers, and even fathers, are at home more. Fathers are welcomed into support groups and have much to offer.

Principal Tip: Perhaps your Parent/Teacher Association could provide donuts and juice for a Boo Hoo breakfast for parents of kindergartners on the first day of school. This provides support and also encourages tearful moms to leave the classroom instead of hovering.

It is the sweet simple things of life which are the real ones after all. ~Laura Ingalls Wilder

Chapter Four
Reading—the Greatest Gift of All

Hugs from Seaver

One day I was substituting in a classroom that had a six-year-old boy named Seaver who was fighting cancer. Seaver did not come to school often, or for long periods, because he was in a lot of pain and did not have much energy. But on this particular day, Seaver came to school. The children were excited to see him. Some gave him high-fives and some gave him hugs. All were gentle with this fragile sweet child.

Seaver sat at his desk for about an hour then asked if his mom could come and get him. He was tired. I let the office know and his beautiful, caring mother came to pick him up from school. I never saw Seaver again. He lost his bravely fought battle with cancer later that year.

Seaver's family and teachers did not want Seaver to be forgotten. His six short years were precious to many. Seaver's kindergarten teacher, Mrs. McDonald, instigated the idea of children donating gently used books. Mrs. McDonald was inspired to call the project *Hugs from Seaver* because she knew Seaver loved being hugged as books were read to him.

Parents were notified of the project. A sign was put in the hallway with a goal of reaching five feet. The first week, the stack reached six feet. The next week, another stack reached six feet. A teacher from another school heard about it and started the project at her school. Our district encouraged other schools to participate.

Volunteers read the books and taped comprehension questions in the back. The books were put in a bag with a picture of Seaver explaining the reading program. Children took the books home and shared the reading/questioning time with their parents. When they were returned, children took another *Hugs from Seaver* book home. Seaver's mother visited all the classes she could to teach other children the love of reading and about the *Hugs from Seaver* program.

Seaver will never be forgotten. It has been over ten years since the loss of Seaver in this world but the program continues today. I'm sure he is smiling down on the lives he has touched. Many children have benefited from this program in more ways than just reading. Seaver's mother went back to school and earned a degree. Seaver's father had shaved his hair when Seaver underwent chemotherapy. His hair has grown back. He and his fire fighter friends continue to heal and help others. A little tree stands in front of the school in memory of this great soul who is still helping others experience the closeness and joy that comes through sharing books.

Have you snuggled next to a child with a book today? I promise you these memories will last and become more precious as time goes by.

My proudest teaching accomplishment was helping children learn to read. It is priceless to see a child's eyes light up when they realize they are truly reading on their own. The gift of reading continues throughout a lifetime. Something about everything can be learned through reading. It is inspiring to know of people who were denied an education, but given the opportunity they learn to read in their senior years. The desire is phenomenal and is not quenched unless achieved.

> *Some women have a weakness for shoes... I can go barefoot if necessary. I have a weakness for books.* ~Oprah Winfrey

When Is a Child Ready to Read?

The debate continues as to when a child is ready to read. When I began teaching kindergarten, the curriculum required teaching the names of the letters. Then teaching the sounds was required. A few short years later, teaching reading was required. When I retired from teaching kindergarten, the curriculum included reading groups with goals of reading at a level that was previously assigned to first grade. The pressure was on for kindergartners to read. And it wasn't just the little ones who felt the pressure.

Previously, it was believed by many that the brain is not ready to read until the age of five. Professionals thought the eyes, brain, and body could not focus on print at preschool age. But we know of children who are reading at age two. How does this happen? It begins at home. Children who are exposed to thousands of hours of reading before entering school are at a clear advantage from those who are less fortunate. Even babies enjoy the closeness experienced while someone holds them on their lap and reads to them. Children capture the love of reading from their family. Not all children will read before entering school, even with exposure, but those who have been frequently read to have a huge and obvious advantage.

My husband did not attend kindergarten as it was not required at that time. Yet he scored as the highest reader in his fifth grade class. He was reading at a college level. His parents were too poor to afford a television but they made frequent trips to the library.

My daughter Sarah was born prematurely. She has a seizure disorder and developmental delays. When she was a toddler, I read to her every night. It was a comforting routine. I was not a teacher at that time. I just knew it was supposed to be good for her. I went back to school to earn my teaching certificate after she was born because I wanted to help her through the special education process. I learned about phonics and we practiced the sounds. It worked. She enjoys reading every day now, just like her father and me.

In a different home environment, with different parents, my daughter might never have learned to read. She is now twenty and reads at a fifth grade level which is higher than many adults. I still have the book *Big Bird Goes to the Park*. We wore it out. It was torn and taped numerous times because it was her favorite book. Sometimes, I wondered if I would lose my mind reading the same book over and over. But I am glad that I did. We shared snuggle and enrichment time, both of which are priceless.

I cannot live without books! ~Thomas Jefferson

Reading is Magical

I highly recommend Mem Fox's book *Reading Magic* for both parents and teachers. She is the author of numerous children's books including *Hattie and the Fox, Koala Lou,* and *Possum Magic.* Fox states, "I love reading it aloud with lots of verve and noise in a sing song, very rhythmic, chanting style." You can visit her informative web and listen to her read books with a delightful Australian accent at www.memfox.net.

Fox is an expert in teaching children to learn to read. She advises spending many hours reading books to children with enthusiasm, musical rhyme, expression and game playing, i.e. fun. Her advice is simplified into three words: rhythm, rhyme and repetition. Fox believes that if parents read aloud a minimum of three stories a day to the young children in their lives, we could probably wipe out illiteracy within one generation.

These books are recommended for rhyme and rhyming on Classroomtalk.com: *Jazz Baby* by Lisa Wheeler, *Sleepyhead Bear* by Lisa Westberg Peters and *Rattletrap Car* by Phyllis Root.

Some kindergartners enter school already reading. Some don't know the letter *A* when their name is Aaron. Five year olds begin kindergarten at staggering degrees of readiness. It is absolutely fine that a child is not reading before entering kindergarten. But it has become strongly recommended in many school districts that a child is reading by the end of kindergarten. A child may be retained in kindergarten who is not reading at a certain level, especially if they are immature.

Brain Development

Fox is an advocate of early childhood stimulation for growth. In her books, she states, "Brain research has revealed that the early years of life are critical to a child's development. Children's brains are only 25 percent developed at birth. From that moment, whenever a baby is fed, cuddled, played with, talked to, sung to, or read to, the other 75 percent of its brain begins to develop. The more stimulation the baby has through its senses of touch, taste, smell, sight, and hearing, the more rapidly that development will occur."

Children need to have loving, laughing, deep and meaningful conversations with adults long before they turn three. A child's IQ development is a reflection of their preschool agenda. There is no argument among professionals that children whose parents have read thousands of hours to them before entering school are at a clear advantage.

Exposure to educational television shows is helpful. But a television does not react, talk back to a child, or answer their inquisitive questions. Children need to learn to express themselves using words, words and more words. In other words, talk to your child and listen while they talk back—communicate. Answer those endless questions. When they are a teenager they'll want to distance themselves from you. Building closeness in the early years will help retain that bonding during the hormonal years when you'll wonder, w*hose child is this?*

Bond through Books

Time spent reading together provides clear evidence to a child of a parent's love, care and focused attention. Children deprived of such time never reach their full potential. They feel inadequate, or even unloved, and may suffer years feeling unconnected. I know of no better way to connect to your child than to snuggle, read together and talk to each other. This is called bonding and is desperately needed in our technologically advanced society.

My daughter just passed the teen years and we still read the scriptures together. This is like a permanent glue to hold a family together.

Routine, Ritual, Ready-to-Read Time

People do better with a routine. Children crave stability which promotes security and a feeling of safety. Devise a ritual of reading together in the same place at the same time. Bedtime is best because it leaves your child feeling loved before sleeping. Even adults will benefit from this reading ritual. Take a deep breath and be with your child in the moment. Put other thoughts and worries aside. Enjoy this special time.

Experts recommend reading three books together each night. I say don't read any if you, or your child, are too tired, or ill, because it can become a power struggle. But every night, when possible, read with your child.

Three categories of books to read are: a book for learning about animals or science, a book of rhyming, and a book of the child's choice even if you do most, or all, of the reading. A child may choose the same book over and over. Read it again and again. Memorization is one of the beginning stages of reading. Repetition instills security in a child; a much needed treasure in our fast-paced world.

Parent/Child Reading Time

It is never too early to begin reading to your child. Some parents read to their child while they are in the womb. We've all heard of musical prodigies whose parents played Mozart for a lift in IQ before the baby was born, revealing that neuron connections are being formed before birth.

With your baby sitting on your lap, begin reading and feeling material books that can be washed. Inexpensive material books can be purchased which have interesting flaps or gadgets attached. Look for thick hard books that have different textures for a child to feel and associate with a word.

After your child starts talking, find a picture book without words. Ask your child to tell you the story based on what they see. This builds thinking and comprehension skills. Or ask your child to tell you the story using their own words from books you have read to them. Did they understand the book? Can they tell you what happened? Who was their favorite character? How did the book make them feel? Was it funny or amazing?

Parents can help their children learn environmental print. Point and say letters, numbers, shapes, and words as you drive or take a walk. You will be surprised what children will remember the next time you pass that way. Words are on cereal boxes, buildings, transportation signs, billboards, newspaper comics, game instructions, grocery lists, bubble bath, toys, everywhere. Praise them for their accomplishments.

Run your finger under the word and say the label before giving your child something from a box or container. This will help your child learn that reading is from left to right and from top to bottom.

Most importantly, let your child see that you enjoy reading and writing. Take children's books with you for those slow times at the doctor's office. You will have fewer behavior problems if your child is actively engaged. Also, keep children's books in the car along with crayons and tablets. If you don't want melted crayons in your car, let your child use colored pencils.

How many parents have sighed as their children scream at a McDonald's golden arch? That arch means food and fun. A kindergartener told me she liked going to the "W" store which one assumes meant Walmart. Denise, my niece, was surprised when her three year old read *zoo* on a poster board. She read hundreds of books to her children before they entered school. It was obvious to their teachers.

> *A book shut tightly, is but a block*
> *of paper.* ~Japanese proverb

The Reading /Writing Connection

The reading/writing connection is essential and speeds up the process of reading. Let your child see you writing. This art is being left unseen with the onset of computers. Give meaning to your writing for the child to witness, and participate in, whenever possible. When your child is interested, help him or her write, copy, or trace a grocery list or a list of errands. Let them cross off the list as it is accomplished. This gives meaning to the written word.

Help your child print a list of Things to Do, a note to dad, a letter to grandmother, or a thank you note to a teacher. These notes are appreciated, proudly displayed and usually read to the class.

One of the best gifts I received was a long note written by a parent explaining to me why she thought I was the best kindergarten teacher for her child. The child had written something on the note too, "I love you. You are my favorite teacher." I kept it to read on those days when I wondered if I was inadequate or insane to teach kindergarten.

I often had children tell me that I was their favorite teacher. Sometimes I would say, "Have you had any other teachers?"

They would usually reply, "No, but I know you are the best."

That was the beauty and reward of teaching kindergarten. Five and six year olds love their teacher unconditionally. They look at their teacher with great admiration at the many things he or she can do. Teaching is a grand adventure of learning together.

Reading Programs

The debate still continues on which reading program is best. I suspect this issue will never be fully resolved. Personally, I believe in teaching the sounds of lower case letters rather than emphasizing the names of the letters. Teach lower case letters first because most print is in lower case. Run your finger under words slowly pronouncing the sounds. Then blend.

Some reading programs call for learning a letter each week beginning with A and ending with Z. I feel a reading program that begins teaching the most frequently used letters and sounds promotes learning to read at a faster rate. There are many phonics programs designed in this context.

Parents can purchase phonic programs if they wish although much is offered for free on the Internet. Zoophonics is highly recommended by researcher and author Carol S. Fitzpatrick who wrote *Help, I Can't*

Read. Free phonics cards are available on www.mes-english.com/phonics.

Teachers must use the school's curriculum and purchased reading program. But good teachers foster reading using every tool that works. Children and adults learn differently. There are visual learners, auditory learners, and sensory/motor/integration learners. Teaching by using all of the five senses creates enthusiastic readers. But remember content is the key. Children must be interested in the book!

Sam I Am

Yes, there really was a Dr. Seuss. He was not an official doctor, but his prescription for fun has delighted readers for more than 60 years. Theodor Seuss Geisel was born on March 2, 1904, in Springfield, Massachusetts. He was an artist and cartoonist but had more to offer. He married Helen Palmer who encouraged him to illustrate and write children's books using use rhythm and rhyme.

Houghton Mifflin and Random House asked Geisel to write a children's primer using 220 new-reader vocabulary words; the end result was *The Cat in the Hat*. Later he was challenged to write a children's book using 50 words or less, prompting the creation of *Green Eggs and Ham*.

The words *Sam I Am* are used many times in the book *Green Eggs and* Ham and provide a wonderful teacher tool for beginner readers. S is a fun letter to teach. Children enjoy making the sssssss sound while sssssssssslithering like a sssssssssssnake. Ask the children for other words that have that beginning sound. As the children think of a word, excitedly print the word on the board as if the class had won a trip to the moon. Use lots of praise and drama. Draw a clue picture beside the word. Together, every day repeat the words as you run a stick under the letters from left to right. Most children are not able to read the words, but they will gradually grasp the concept of a word. They will eventually realize letters are important because so much time and energy are spent reinforcing them. It is especially beneficial if parents are sharing in the enthusiasm.

The next letter of the week could be M. The M sound can be learned using M&M's for taste, patterning and counting. Dissolving M&M's in one's mouth connects the mmmmm sound. Children enjoy placing M&Ms on paper to form their name.

Some schools are mandating how many days teachers can offer sugary treats in their classroom. Our school district had a three day limit on parties or holiday celebrations. But I was fortunate to have an understanding principal who closed her eyes if the children occasionally ate food, including sweets, for a learning experience. If my principal walked in my room while the children were using sweats as a learning tool, she would smile and say, "Eat the evidence." These are five year olds we're teaching to read. If it works, use it.

Now that the children recognize the letter S and the letter M, it is time to teach the word *Sam*. *Green Eggs and Ham* can be read joyously emphasizing the words *Sam I Am*. Encourage the children to participate in the reading, as you run your finger under the print.

Print *Sam I A* on the board. Have the children draw a picture of a character that could be in this book. Encourage them to print the words *Sam I Am* under their drawing as best they are able. Help them print words by making dots they can connect. Or print the words and have them trace it in "rainbow colors" which means tracing the letters several times in different colors.

Kindergarten is a time for celebrating every theme and holiday permissible. Put theme words on the board with picture clues. Encourage the children to draw something pertaining to the theme and to write words below their picture. I was astonished at how fast some children were able to write sentences using the words on the board.

> When I get a little money I buy books, and if any is left, I buy food. ~Disiderius Erasmus

Reading Groups

Reading or literacy groups are formed in kindergarten after a period of adjustment to school. Small groups of children read the same book together and then take it home to read with a parent. I remember five-year-old Hailey telling me in an embarrassed voice, "I can't read". No child should feel ashamed because they aren't reading in kindergarten. But even memorization is a beginning stage of reading.

"Yes, you can read, Hailey. Let's read it together." I pointed to each word and slowly moved my finger under the word and across the page. Then I pointed to the picture. "I see a spider. I see a bat. I see a flower. I see a hat."

We read the book together. Then Hailey read the book back to me by herself. This memorization process went on for weeks. I wasn't really sure if Hailey was reading by herself or not. She heard other children reading the same books over and over again. I wondered if perhaps she had just memorized them. But one day, Hailey sounded out a word by herself. I was ecstatic.

I said, "Hailey, you are reading!" She looked at me with astonishment and a glow in her eyes that would be hard to forget. Hailey knew she had finally learned how to read.

What Works

Does whole language work? Do phonics programs work? Does exposure and repetition work? Does labeling every noun in the room work? Are word attack skills required? Does hopping in patterns work? Is memorization of sight words necessary? Does reading nursery rhymes help? Yes, yes, yes... Whatever works is recommended. Have the children experience learning using the five senses and you'll be a much loved teacher or parent. Make it fun. These are five and six year olds who are eager to please adults. Take advantage of that while you can.

Put together blocks with each sound of a word to build the concept of a word. Stretch a rubber band as you slowly say a word emphasizing each sound. Stamp your feet while rhyming, saying syllables, or making patterns. Clap to each syllable of a word. Physical rhythmic movement combined with visual and auditory stimuli promote reading.

During my years of teaching, I attended numerous workshops on reading. There are many guaranteed reading programs. I believe it boils down to this: repetition, repetition, repetition with huge doses of enthusiasm, excitement, praise and fun. Reading is accomplished by learning the sounds of the letters and blending the sounds.

- Teaching lower case letters first is best because most words are printed in lower case
- Slowly blend the sounds together
- Memorizing "sight" words is helpful because they appear often in print and promote fluency of reading which increases comprehension
- Content and fun illustrations are key. Offer a variety and use what is of interest to the child.

Help children learn a sight word a week. Put the Word of the Week in the parent newsletter for reinforcement at home. For struggling students, print the sight word on an index card to include in the weekly folder sent home.

Comprehension

Children should be asked comprehension questions about what they have read or heard you read: What happened? Who was the story about? What was the story about? What did they like about the book? How did it make them feel? You will be entertained with their answers. Always respond positively when a child answers a question, or they may not want to answer a question again for weeks.

Put paint, markers and play dough in centers (which may be called *stations* or even *corrals* in Texas). This is play/learning group time when children are free to do what they want, within reason, in a small structured group which offers certain materials. The centers in my classroom were labeled Home, Library, Paint, Blocks, Games, and Computer. Children were allowed to choose which center they wanted each day. I allowed the well behaved children, or those who stayed on green, the reward of choosing first. The exception was the Computer Center. It was in such high demand that the children were given the opportunity to use it when their name was called by alphabetical order. They learned their name quickly where it was posted on the behavior board as they anticipated their turn and made sure I didn't miss calling their name.

Perhaps a child just wants to play with plastic dinosaurs during center time. That is fine. They are learning to share, make friends, and use their imagination. But I was surprised, and saddened, that many children are not allowed to use crayons, markers, paint, play dough or scissors at home, probably because the parent does not want to supervise. Preschoolers can use them effectively with supervision. They will love you for letting them. See Chapter Nine for play dough recipes.

Joke: A kindergarten teacher received the following Absence Excuse Note: "Please excuse Sammy from school last Friday. He had very loose vowels."

Compare and Contrast with the Venn Diagram

John Venn conceived the Venn diagram around 1880. The concept is to link items by characteristics or attributes. Items can be visually demonstrated as having something in common such as comparing people, animals, places, events, and ideas.

Kindergarteners can understand the concept of same and different by letting them physically manipulate objects. Place two hula hoops on the floor and let children sort objects such as plastic food and animals. Then they could sort animals by which live in a zoo and which live on a farm. Do any of the animals live in both places? Overlap the hoops and have the children put those animals in the middle section.

Later in the school year, books can be used to compare and contrast. Draw two huge circles on the whiteboard intersecting them to form three sections. Write the titles of the two books above the end sections. Write the word *Same* over the middle section. You can compare and contrast these books by Laura Joffe Numeroff:

If You give a Mouse a Cookie and *If You Give Moose a Muffin*

If You Give a Pig a Pancake and *If You Give a Cat a Cupcake*

If You Take a Mouse to School and *If You Take A Mouse to the Movies*

These fun books are also loved by the students and are good for Venn Diagrams:

The Giant Turnip and *The Enormous Carrot*
The Mitten Tree and *The Giving Tree*

The Gingerbread Baby and *The Gingerbread Man*
The Mitten and *The Hat*

It takes several attempts before the children understand the concept of same and different in books. But during the process they observe meaning of the written word and eventually they understand *same* and *different*. It is rewarding to witness their progress.

Teaching the concept of opposites is more easily grasped especially with movement accompanying words such as tall, short; big, little; left, right; top, bottom; high, low; out, in; and over, under.

Favorite Books

Children love books that are funny. Who doesn't need to let off a little pressure by laughing? My students begged me to read David Shannon's books including *No David!*, *David Goes to School* and *Duck on a Bike*.

I love Jamie Lee Curtis' books including *When I Was Little*, *Big Words for Little People*, *Is There Really a Human Race?*, *It's Hard to be Five*, *Today I Feel Silly*, *Tell Me Again about the Night I was Born* (about adoption).

With over thirty seven million books in print, Jan Brett is one of the nation's foremost author illustrators of children's books including *The Mitten*, *Gingerbread Baby*, *Armadillo Rodeo*, and many other fabulous books. She loves hedgehogs and has several for pets. Her web, www.janbrett.com, offers numerous activities, coloring sheets, computer games, printable games, lesson plans and educational ideas for your classroom.

The Three Billy Goats Gruff is a fun book for the children to listen to when read with a great deal of expression. Children's books should be ready slowly enough for comprehension and with grandiose animation. Let them participate when possible, such as voicing when the goats tramp over the bridge.

Many authors of children's books have excellent webs with activities, worksheets and games. Some even offer a link to listen to the author reading their own books. If your voice needs a break, you can turn the pages as the author reads. Listed are some authors' webs with a book title:

- www.seussville.com: *Green Eggs and Ham*
- www.lauranumeroff.com: *If you Give a Mouse a Cookie*
- www.scholastic.com/titles/nodavid/davidshann on: *No David!*
- www.jamieleecurtisbooks.com: *It's Hard to Be Five*
- www.eric-carle.com: *The Very Hungry Caterpillar*
- www.robertmunsch.com: *Love You Forever*

Reading Rockets is a powerhouse of information on teaching reading for parents and teachers. Visit their web at www.readingrockets.org.

However defined, a healthy self-esteem must be carefully fostered in our youngsters if they are to realize, and eventually assume, all the promises and challenges that life sets before them. ~Jamie Lee Curtis

Sad Statistics

A 2007 report from the United Nations Educational, Scientific and Cultural Organizations lists the United States of America as ranking 21 in worldwide literacy. Statistics can be maneuvered and misrepresented but the National Assessment of Adult Literacy through the U.S Department of Education has also released sad statistics. An extensive government study showed that 21% to 23% of adult Americans were not "able to locate information in text," could not "make low-level inferences using printed materials," and were unable to "integrate easily identifiable pieces of information."

Statistics posted by Central Connecticut State University were startling:
- 1/3 of high school graduates (after receiving their diplomas) will never read another book for the rest of their lives.
- Forty-two percent of college graduates never read another book after college.
- 80% of U.S. adults have not been in a bookstore in the last five years.
- Most readers do not get past page 18 in a book they have purchased.
- Customers 55 and older account for one-third of all books purchased.

Many of the adults considered in these statistics went to school before special testing and services were offered for dyslexia and other learning disabilities. If your child is in the second semester of first grade and still not reading, consult their teacher and request testing if the teacher has not already offered it.

> *The man who does not read good books has no advantage over the man who cannot read them.* ~Mark Twain

Computer Webs offering Worksheets, Activities and Games

It can be amazing, inspiring, and educational to use what is free on the Internet. You can google *phonics reading games, abc song,* and authors' webs for free information, worksheets, activities, games and educational ideas. I like these two sites for free worksheets and printable books:
www.beginningreading.com
www.abcteach.com

Computer Games and Activities

Starfall.com
Earobics.com/gamegoo
ABC songs
Kids.yahoo.com
Billybear4kids.com
PBSkids.org
scholastic.com/parents/play/games/
Kidnercorner.com
Enchantedlearning.com
Drjean.org
Blackdog4kids.com
Seussville.com

Television as a Teaching Tool

Sesame Street
Read Between the Lions
Word World
Pinky Dinky Doo
Wilbur
Blue's Room and Blue's Clues
Super Why!
Word girl
The Electric Company
Sid the Science Kid
Curious George

Top Rated Kinderarten Blog

This kindergarten teachers's blog leads you to 100 other kinder blogs: aplacecalledkindergarten.blogspot.

> *What makes a curious reader?*
> *You do.* ~Curious George poster

Note to Parents

Love and cherish your child. Time is the most precious thing to spend on a child. Find inexpensive things to do together like going to the library or park and playing outside in the yard. Buy puzzles and educational toys at garage sales to keep your child's mind active and to foster creativity. Staring at a television does not foster creativity or survival skills. Television and computers can facilitate learning but they do not answer a child's many questions about their exciting world. Balance is necessary for developing the mind. Exercise and fresh air are needed desperately as more children become obese sitting in front of immobile screens.

Teacher and Parent Tip: Write grants to obtain books and educational tools. I co-wrote four grants which were funded for big books, literacy center books, and science tools. Science books seemed to spark the most interest. Our world is fascinating to children.

A Cautionary Note

I would like to caution parents to not stress themselves, or their child, if their kindergartner is not reading. Jean Piaget, respected theorist on the stages of child development, believed:

1. not all children are ready to read at the same age and in the same manner,
2. not all children are ready to read by the first grade,
3. not all children learn in the same manner, and
4. reading is a great deal more than decoding printed symbols on a page and mouthing words.

According to Piaget, hurrying a child through a stage will not speed up brain growth, but it may deprive a child of the proper experiences needed for secure sequential development. The following section explains Piaget's stages of child development. Appropriate activities will promote learning but pushing, or skipping, stages is not advisable and may even be harmful if not impossible. Please let children be children.

Piaget's Stages of Child Development

Sensorimotor—from birth to about age two. During this stage, the child learns about himself and his environment through motor and reflex actions. Thought derives from sensation and movement. The child learns that he is separate from his environment. Peek a Boo becomes a favorite game as children learn people and things continue to exist even though out of the reach of their senses. Teaching a child in this stage should be geared to the sensorimotor system. Touchy-feeling books are loved by toddlers. You can modify behavior by using the senses. A frown, a stern or soothing voice serve as appropriate techniques.

Preoperational begins about the time the child starts to talk to about age seven. Applying the new knowledge of language, children begin to use symbols to represent objects. Early in this stage they also personify objects. Children are better able to think about things and events that aren't immediately present. Oriented to the present, the child has difficulty conceptualizing time. Thinking is influenced by fantasy or the way they'd like things to be. Children assume that others see situations from their viewpoint. Children like using the five senses in order to play an active role in learning.

Concrete learning is from about first grade to early adolescence. The child develops an ability to think abstractly and to make rational judgments about concrete or observable phenomena, which in the past he needed to manipulate physically to understand. Children need to be given the opportunity to ask questions and to explain things back to you

Formal Operations occurs during adolescence. The teenager no longer requires concrete objects to make rational judgments. At his point, he is capable of hypothetical and deductive reasoning.

> *A capacity, and taste, for reading, gives access to whatever has already been discovered by others. It is the key, or one of the keys, to the already solved problems. And not only so. It gives a relish, and facility, for successfully pursuing the [yet] unsolved ones . ~Abraham Lincoln*

Donate Books

Bestselling author David Baldacii (The Camel Club Series) and his wife, Michelle, started the Wish You Well Foundation. On their web, Baldacci writes, "Imagine your daily life, the information you process, the decisions you make based on that process and the actions you take based upon your decisions. Now imagine doing all these things while either being unable to read or reading at a below-average level. Well, you've successfully imagined the daily lives of nearly 100 million people, half the population of the United States. A country that was founded on the principles of free speech, free press, and the freedom of religion—all rights tied inexorably to words—is fast becoming an illiterate nation. The ability to read is the foundation for everyday life. Indeed, virtually none of the major issues we face as a nation today can be successfully overcome until we eradicate illiteracy. That's why we created the Wish You Well Foundation®.

Perhaps your favorite author or actor has started a program to donate books. You could look on their web for information or contact your local library. The following people, or programs, promote literacy:

- Nancy Robinson Masters: Paperbacks for Patriots through the Commemorative Air at www.commemorativeairforce.org

- Barbara Bush: Foundation for Family Literature: www.barbarabushfoundation.com
- Dolly Parton: Imagination Station Library: www.imaginationlibrary.com
- Laura Bush Foundation (grants available for school libraries): www.laurabushfoundation.org
- The Library of Congress Curious George Campaign: www.read.gov

The home is the child's first school, the parent is the child's first teacher, and reading is the child's first subject. ~Barbara Bush

Chapter Five
Science—Survival Specials

Have you ever noticed how large a child's eye is when a magnifying glass is held close? Can you imagine what the child is seeing? What is the child hearing? Will they touch a live worm or an owl pellet? Children are not bored when learning science.

What Does It Take to Be Alive?

We'd been over and over what it takes for organisms to be alive. It was required kindergarten teaching. I did my best to demonstrate these properties and to help the children memorize this important information into their sponge-like brains.

Once again, I asked, "What do organisms need to be alive?"

Toby was born premature. He was diagnosed with ADHD at the tender age of four but was not taking any medicine. My eyes opened with surprise as Toby raised his hand. This was unusual but it was Spring, after all.

"Yes, Toby. Thank you for raising your hand." *Will kindergarten miracles never cease?* "What do things need to be alive?" I repeated for the distracted children.

"They need to be a cowboy," proudly answered Toby who was wearing cowboy boots even though tennis shoes were strongly recommended.

This was Texas, after all. *What was I thinking? To teach something needs air, water, food and sunlight?* Being a cowboy, or cowgirl, to feel alive on a horse, was definitely a much cooler response. We all smiled and no one rebuked Toby's honest answer.

Worms, Worms and More Worms

The Science Fair was approaching. The teachers had been warned and encouraged to attend science workshops. Now it was time to act. What would be our classroom science project this year? I knew that whatever it was, it had to be performed and recorded on three occasions to follow the scientific rules. Cheating was not an option. The children knew the concept of three.

I asked the children for ideas which I dutifully wrote on the board hoping they would see the connection between the spoken word and written word.

No one seemed to have any great ideas. I wondered if that was due to too much television, Nintendo, Playstation, Wii, Xbox, etc. I said, "Let's think about it and do this again tomorrow." Surely, I was a better science teacher than these ideas portrayed. I had attended numerous science workshops, after all.

I asked my husband if he had any ideas. He responded with one word, "Worms."

"Worms?" I was proud of my science curriculum but did not particularly like worms.

"Yup, do something with worms. Then I can use them for fishing bait after the experiment," he explained.

"Worms?" I imagined touching slimy worms. Yuk! "I think after this year, I'll retire."

"Put 'em in a box with three different kinds of dirt. See which kind they like best."

"But we have to count them...three times!" Double yuk. I made a sour face. I'd grown up with two older mischievous brothers but wasn't sure I was eager for a worm experiment.

My husband wasn't ready for me to retire. His enthusiasm grew. "I'll go to the garden store and get you a trailer full of composted dirt. We need some for the flower beds anyway. You could use good old Texas clay-dirt and then a mixture both. I'll buy you some worms at the bait shop."

I could see the fishing reels spinning in his brain. He had a mission and a legitimate reason to go fishing. I didn't accompany him on fishing trips but his best friend loved it. Whenever I asked my husband what he and his buddy talked about he responded, "Nothing. We're fishing." That's all the glimpse I had of this sacred commune with nature.

Occasionally, I felt sorry for the worms and the fish. But Dan rarely brought back fish. According to Dan, "The fish are thrown back into the lake if they're small. That way they can grow bigger." *Yeah, right. Show me the fish.*

When Dan did bring back fish, he cleaned and fried them. *Maybe I'll get some fresh fried fish as my reward for playing with worms. Oh, Joy.*

The next day, I again asked the children for more ideas for our science project. Some answers involved dinosaurs, volcanoes and horses. I said, "Would you like to learn what kind of dirt worms like to live in?" Squeals filled the room. Some children clapped and some made horrible faces but they were all excited. I'd hit a home run.

I told a few worried girls that they did not have to touch the worms. They could help count and observe. I promised to ask the school nurse for sanitary gloves.

I bought three plastic containers with lids. My husband proudly brought me three dozen wiggly worms and my flower beds were replenished with the leftover compost. I certainly did not need a trailer full for our experiment. I put the dirt into the containers and hauled it to the school building, again feeling grateful I had kept my daughter's wagon.

It was time to begin the experiment. The children dressed in their white science lab coats which I had earned for them through many hours of attending teacher science workshops. Our district was trying to increase science scores and teachers were rewarded for taking classes. I also had earned magnifying glasses, goggles, weights and science books. I'm not sure the goggles helped the children count the worms but the children looked very impressive in their lab coats, gloves and goggles.

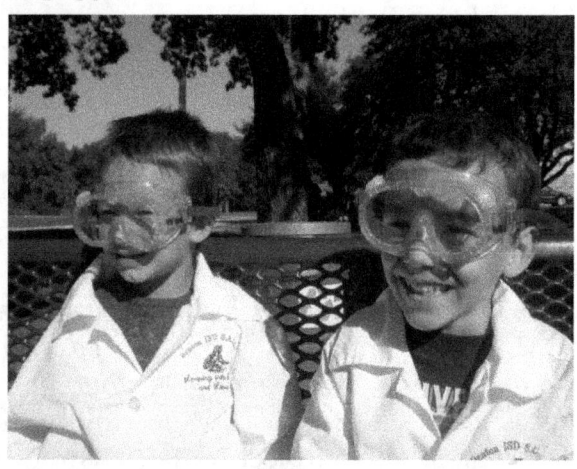

One girl named Kelsey loved counting the worms. She had struggled in my classroom and cried at the drop of a pencil. Finally, her parents put her on medicine for Attention Deficit Hyperactivity Disorder (ADHD) and she was beginning to settle into the routine. If it took worms to build her self-esteem then I was happy we'd discovered that fact.

The children counted, charted and recorded how many worms survived in the three containers. This was done on three different days. I was worn out but proud that we had accomplished a true science experiment. More worms survived in composted dirt than in Texas clay dirt or in a combination of the two. Our chart supported our theory. With my help, the children painstakingly printed the theory, hypotheses and results.

We proudly displayed our experiment in the cafeteria hoping no worms escaped or were eaten by a preschooler of a touring family. Judges came from the district to see the experiments. The next day, it was announced on the loud speaker that my class won first place for kindergarten! We received cupcakes and a trophy. My husband went fishing with some large wiggly worms. And I had my picture taken wearing a smile and my lab coat while holding a worm.

What Happens to a Mealworm?

Another student favorite science theme is that of studying the life of a mealworm. There is truly an amazing array of academic materials to correlate with the lessons plans on mealworms. I assume these were achieved by some bi-polar teacher, energized during the mania time, or possibly a first year teacher who drank too much caffeine and had no children at home.

We had been doing our best to grow, feed, count, race and even reproduce mealworms. I'd about had it and longed for the day free of worms. However, we weren't finished yet. One of my more obedient girls would not sit down during circle time. She appeared glued to the mealworm container.

"Monica, please join us at circle time," I asked yet again.

"But there's a strange looking bug in with our worms," she drawled, Texas style.

Of course, all the children lunged up and sprinted toward the container.

"What, where, why?" was heard in unison as they pushed to get a closer look.

"All right, let me see, please." I managed to grab the container and lift it higher than the children. In the excitement, or due to pressure of children's bodies, I let it go. Oatmeal, mealworms and one lone beetle dropped to the floor. Now screams added to the excitement.

It is not easy to clean up oatmeal and mealworms from carpet, especially with twenty-two eager children wanting to help. One boy grabbed the lone beetle. I begged him to be gentle but it was soon squashed. It was time for the "Be Kind to Creatures" lecture. Out came the big book on beetles for a scientific journey through the life of a worm.

Teacher Tale: One day I was sitting in the assistant principal's office having a serious discussion about a child with behavior problems. His phone rang. He listened then told me, "I'll be right back."

I waited about ten minutes when he returned. He said, "One of the fifth grader's insects on their science poster board was still alive."

I knew things grew bigger in Texas but wondered what kind of insect would cause the teacher to call for assistance.

Teacher Tip: Recycle, reuse, replenish, restore. Learning comes from hand-on experiences. Children who are not necessarily successful at paper work can shine when it comes to counting worms.

Write grants to obtain science books. Ask your principal or district staff to give you information on grant suppliers. Take science seminars so that you can quote research to write into the grant request, stating the importance of science and how it integrates with other subjects. Perhaps a parent is willing to write a grant for your classroom or your grade level.

The Five Senses

Google *The Five Senses* for wonderful preschool and kinder activities that will stimulate the mind and body for sensory motor integration. A good children's science web is www.enchantedlearning.com.

I hear, and I forget. I see, and I remember. I do, and I understand. ~Chinese Proverb

Do you need some quiet time? Encourage the children to use their imaginations and **hear** different sounds like a breeze blowing, a falling leaf, a volcano, dreaming, humming, laughing, sneezing, whistling, an ice cube, the ocean, a river, a cave, a drop of rain, eating an apple, sleeping, crying, singing, animal noises, breathing and anything else imaginable.

Children love to **feel** objects. One of the most fun things for them to do is clean their desk with shaving cream. This process takes off crayon marks and germs. I've seen children roll their fingers and hands over crayons for a long time just to feel them. Play-Doh is an important part of kindergarten. Many children are not allowed to use it at home. See Chapter Nine for play dough recipes.

Children enjoy the sense of **smell**. Put different scents into baggies or jars and pass them around. They could smell vanilla extract, perfumes, flowers, onions, Lavender, vinegar (pickles) and scented oils.

Let them **taste** different items that are salty (pretzels), sour (lemons, pickles), sweet (candy) and bitter (olives).

Children love to **see** bright colors. Let them paint. It is messy and they must be taught to put the red paintbrush back into the red container and not share it with other colors. Take them outside to paint with water. Let them paint with Q-tips and white paint on black paper. Always have them wear an apron in the art center when painting and always supervise.

> *Life is a big canvas, throw all the paint on it you can.* ~Danny Kaye

It Is What It Is

"Teacher, why is the moon so bright at night?"

Here was yet another teaching opportunity. I promptly got out my flashlight, a big ball and a smaller ball. I asked a fidgety student to turn off the lights. I could feel the excitement mount.

"Robin, that is an excellent question. Please come hold this big ball and pretend you are our earth." Robin was eager to oblige

"Mason, please hold the flashlight. You are the sun." Mason began beaming as brightly as the sun.

"This small ball I am holding is the moon. The moon orbits around the earth. See how the sun is shining on it? This is called a full moon. Now when I move the moon behind the earth you can only see part of it. This is called a half moon."

I went into a long explanation about the glories of our galaxy. I wondered if I had ventured too far off orbit when Jordan said, "My mom said God put the moon up there to give us kids some light at night."

Good as any explanation I've ever heard.

If you can't explain it simply, you don't understand it well enough. ~Albert Einstein

Joke: The cross-eyed teacher was having problems at school. She couldn't get her pupils to straighten out.

Grow Garden, Grow

Our school was fortunate to have volunteers make an outdoor garden. Parents cleaned out an area, tilled it, and put in raised beds with good soil. We loved taking our walk after lunch and as a reward often visited the garden and bunnies. My class planted some Iris bulbs and vegetable seeds. One teacher's pumpkin vines grew very long with huge blossoms for the children to admire.

Butterflies like zinnias which require little maintenance. Or plant a "butterfly bush." The Purple Emperor English Butterfly Bush aka *Buddleia* grows well in Southern climates with little water. Shallow bird baths are best and will attract a variety of birds and insects. Pennies in a birdbath can prevent fungi from growing.

Let the children plant bean seeds in a cup. They grow fast and long. Also, put bean seeds in baggies, keep moist and watch them become sprouts. Or sprout seeds in a jar. I found lentil seeds work well and taste good. Soak for one day, then drain but keep seeds moist. Sprouts are a very nutritious inexpensive source of vitamins and protein. See Chapter Nine for the recipe Dirt Pudding.

Joke: A teacher was giving a lesson on the circulation of the blood. Trying to make the matter clearer, she said, "If I stood on my head, the blood would run into it, and I would turn red in the face."
"Yes," the students nodded in agreement
"Then why is it that while I am standing upright in the ordinary position the blood doesn't run into my feet and turn them red?"
A little fellow shouted, "Cuz your feet ain't empty."

Rock Candy

Children love things that move, grow or change. Here is a link for a recipe to make rock candy. The crystals will grow for three to seven days, then may be eaten:
www.chemistry.about.com

Joke: A frustrated father asked, "Why can't we have heaven in our home?"
Sammy yelled, "Because of gravity!"

Painted Lady Butterflies in the Classroom

Spring is a time of birth, including butterflies. The kindergarten teachers order chrysalis every Spring. It is amazing but these undeveloped insects survive the packing and shipping process. We carefully put them into a container with some dirt, leaves and grass. I sprayed the leaves every day for moisture.

The children named our chrysalis Angel, Orangey, Batman and Pokémon. Nothing happened for five days. Then one day, a butterfly started to emerge. Its wings were solid orange and barely flittered. The next day, the children were excited to see more butterflies. We kept them a few days then released them outside. It was inspiring to see the little butterflies rise into the sky. We think we saw them later at the park.

The Ant Farm

How cheap can a science project be? Children love anything that is moving, no matter how small. Put some ants in a large jar and cover it with cheesecloth or some material then secure it tightly with a rubber band. Remind the students to not take the lid off any critter's container. Ants will thrive on any food but like children, they like sweets. Orange and apple slices provide moisture.

Teach the children about cooperation while learning about ant colonies. Read *The Ant Bully* and incorporate character building into your theme. You may be able to watch the movie on a rainy day, giving you a break and the students a reinforcement of the theme.

Joke: The kindergartner brought a praying mantis to school. He asked his teacher, "Do animals pray?"

The teacher replied, "I'm sure the ones in my classroom do."

Owl Pellets—The True Test of a Scientist

No teacher has experienced teaching until their class has dissected owl pellets. If you do this, you can, and will, do anything. What is an owl pellet? It is what an owl coughs up including hair, bones, and rocks. What does an owl eat? Mice, snakes and lizards. You got it, that's what's inside the fur ball pellet. And you and your students are going to have the thrill of taking it apart. The joy of teaching is truly mind boggling.

There will be surprised gasps from parents and students, perhaps even a few protests, when they learn your class will be dissecting owl pellets. Invite parents to participate because you will need all the help offered. Owl pellets are a fantastic example of the food chain, ecology, animal structure, skeletal anatomy and natural history. Most students will not comprehend all this but they will remember dissecting an owl pellet.

You will need lots of glue. Yes, glue. Because you will have a Xeroxed sheet of a mouse skeleton on which the children will glue the tiny bones. Then the parents will be astounded and proud of their little scientist.

Joke: Brittany's fifth grade class had been receiving the "Don't Do Drugs" lessons at school. One day, her science teacher asked the children what they had for dinner the night before, hoping to prompt a lesson on healthy nutrition.

Brittany responded, "We had marijuana steak, baked potatoes and pie."

The science teacher said, "Excuse me. What did you say?"

Brittany repeated, "Marijuana steak. You know, it's soaked overnight."

"Do you mean *marinated* steak?" the teacher asked.

"That's what I said," answered Brittany.

The teacher made a mental note to send home more literature from the "Don't Do Drugs" campaign regarding marijuana. Was this the reason for her parents' blood shot eyes and lack of responsiveness?

Parent Tip: Let your child have a pet. Caring for a goldfish is inexpensive and can encourage responsibility. A hummingbird feeder brings hours of enjoyment for supplying sugar water. Hummers do not need the food coloring. Just add one cup sugar to four cups hot water and let it cool before putting it in your feeder. Keep leftover sugar water in the refrigerator. If your family has allergies, consider taking care of an outdoor cat. They need a place to hide like under a porch or in a garage. But mostly they just want to be petted. Children should wash their hands after petting animals (as good a reason as any).

> *To feed someone, help them grow a garden.* ~ Old Japanese Proverb

Chapter Six
Discipline—Combat Duty or Common Sense Tactics?

Why in Heaven's Name Do You Even Come to School?

"Why do you come to school?" I occasionally asked, usually out of frustration.

If the class looked at me like fawns facing headlights, I would answer, "To learn to read and write and make friends so that you can be happy."

One day, I asked that question as Justin prodded me to take an over-the-counter pain reliever for my pounding headache. I was afraid if the headache didn't go away soon, the principal might find me curled in a fetal position under my desk, sucking my thumb.

Beautiful Mailey Mae with her stylish clothes and long gorgeous curls, dutifully raised her hand showing off her glittery blue fingernails with flower decals.

"Yes, Mailey Mae. Why do parents send their children to school?"

"So you won't be some silly maniac kid," she matter-of-factly answered, nodding so much the curls bounced around her back. I pictured her mother using those exact same words.

I couldn't stop the laugh on that response. I could finally feel my headache subside.

K I S S (Keep It Simple Silly)

Good discipline is caring enough about children to provide, and enforce, fair and simple rules for their protection and learning. Good rules pave the road toward a successful year for you and for the students. I used the following four rules because they could be stretched to cover everything necessary for them to learn and for me to survive.

1. Follow Directions
2. Keep your hands and feet to yourself
3. Finish your work
4. Be kind

Children can help you decide on the classroom rules on the first day of school with the teacher's prompting. They will be more apt to comply when they are part of the formation process. Once the rules are decided upon, write them in big letters on a poster board and read them together the first thing every morning.

The children may not be able to read the rules at the beginning of the school year, but they will memorize them. They love to SHOUT THEM OUT. Never, under any circumstances, change the rules during the school year. You have valid reasons for the rules—so that everyone can be safe and so that everyone can learn. The children will eventually memorize this too. It's a teacher's survival tactic.

TX Bear

At the beginning of each school year, I placed a stuffed bear on a tall cabinet. This was beloved TX Bear. He wore a red neckerchief.

I told the children that this special bear was watching the children to decide whose home he wanted to visit. This caused quite a stir. The week's Super Star would be able to take TX Bear home along with his journal. The student was to draw a picture of what he and TX Bear liked to do. They were also encouraged to write about it with the help of their parents. When they brought the journal and bear back to school, I would proudly show the child's drawing and read what the parent, or child, had written.

The children loved being Super Star but I think they loved taking TX Bear home even more. I put TX Bear in a bag with crayons and a notebook and off he went with the Super Star. I lost many crayons, neckerchiefs, a few bears, and several notebooks, but it was worth it. When a notebook was full, I put it in the classroom library. It was a favorite book for the children to admire and try to read or to find their page of memories.

TX Bear was taken to the park, swung in backyards, jumped on trampolines, slept in bunk beds and taken to grandparents. Occasionally, a parent concerned about germs would give TX Bear a bath in the washing machine. *Good idea.*

Teacher Tip: I bought yards of bandana material that was decorated with horses and cut neckerchiefs for TX Bear. I made neckerchiefs for each child when we studied our great state of Texas. I didn't bother sewing around the edges due to lack of time. Besides, stringy neckerchiefs are cooler. I let the children take the neckerchiefs home. They were thrilled because every child in Texas dreams of horses.

The Marble Jar

I still have parents thank me for giving them the idea to use a marble jar at home. Our classroom marble jar was filled as the class received compliments. These compliments could be earned from me, parents, staff, high school helpers, and substitutes, i.e. anyone 16 or over. I had some larger marbles that were earned if the principal gave a compliment to anyone in the class or the entire class. When the jar was full, my husband and daughter made cupcakes to celebrate. It usually took about a month to fill the jar. We celebrated on a Friday afternoon making Fridays one more reason to be considered *fun*.

The children voted on which kind of cupcake they wanted, including icing. This was a brief lesson in democracy and also demonstrated the reading/writing connection. Some days, the children would beg me to count the marbles. We estimated how many it would take to fill the jar. This is math after all. I never took any marbles out of the jar as punishment even if a child, or the class, got into trouble. The children eagerly looked at the marble jar anticipating glorious cupcakes. But more than that, they knew they had slowly earned those homemade cupcakes.

It only cost a few dollars to make cupcakes and is worth every penny. My husband brought them on that special Friday afternoon. Years later, parents and children see my husband and still refer to him as "The Cupcake Man."

Respect, Responsibility, Reinforcement and Rewards

Discipline means caring enough about a child to help them respect themselves and others by learning to control themselves. Caring deeply about children means you want good-humored control and firm discipline for them. Children should be expected to obey adults, provided the adults are reasonable. Young children are not experienced enough, or emotionally mature enough, to be in charge of themselves over long periods of time. Adults lead children to self-control by reinforcing good behavior and being a role model. It is the responsibility of parents and teachers to teach children self-control. This may not be easy with some children but the rewards are definitely worth the effort.

The good news is that children want limits and boundaries. Consistency and stability are essential ingredients of security. Many children do not feel secure due to single parent families, a transient society, and the economy. I was surprised at how many of my students' parents had already divorced or the mothers had never married. Some kindergartners had no contact with their father. Some had grandparents raising them. Today, families are spread all over our country and maybe even in different parts of the world. It has become even more important for teachers to provide a secure teaching environment. Carol S. Fitzpatrick has worked with children for more than twenty-five years as a teacher, reading specialist and researcher. In her book, *Help, I Can't Read!* Fitzpatrick writes, "Children need boundaries to feel safe. They periodically need to push at the boundaries to be sure they're still there. If the teacher is consistent, then the students feel safe, all is well with the world, and they can go back to work."

Positive reinforcement is the best technique for encouraging wanted behavior. Words, praise, and smiles are preferable to food or anything else and should be used lavishly Some children need more reinforcement than others. Personally, I think it is all right, and found it helpful, to bribe children with cupcakes or a treat starting with the Letter of the Week (see Chapter Nine), a trip to the park, or a movie watched on Friday afternoon (correlating with the lesson plans, of course). I called Fridays *Fun Fridays*. If a parent wanted to send cookies or cupcakes for their child's birthday, I encouraged them to wait until Friday.

Kindergartners love stickers, stamps, candy and special times. A trip to the school garden to pet the rabbits, a movie on Fridays, or a good note home, may be all it takes to motivate a child. Be reasonably open to their suggestions. Let them vote on rewards or movie choices.

I had numerous holiday, animal, and letter stamps. I put stamps and stickers on my Wish List in my newsletter. Children love the scented stamps. If they were doing paperwork at that time, I also stamped their papers if they put their name on it (amazingly difficult to remember for a kindergartner). Every child wanted to earn this prestigious emblem.

Wearing a huge smile, compliment children who are displaying appropriate behavior. Keep M&M's handy. Place one in front of a child who is behaving. It doesn't take long before all the children want an M&M and not just for the flavor. I was amazed at how quiet a room could become with a single M&M placed in front of each child or with a sticker placed on each child's hand.

Young children need action. They need hands-on learning connected to their real world. They learn by exploring and discovering, as evidenced by the enthusiasm of learning through the five senses. You cannot expect a small child to sit for long periods of time. Action and movement will cut down on behavior problems. Keep students busy. Some children will finish their work before others. Down time for active kindergartners can prove to be distractive for students still working. Children should have a notebook and a library book in their desk for those times when they need something to do while others are finishing work. Collect books for your classroom library or subscribe to children's magazines such as *Zoobooks, Ranger Rick, Ladybug,* and *Your Big Backyard.* Put this on your Wish List in your newsletter.

Teacher Tip: Be sure a Friday movie coincides with your weekly theme, is in the lesson plans, and that the principal approves. Parents may not appreciate certain movies shown at school or for the entire movie to be watched at one time. Perhaps you can record "Word World" or "Between the Lions" for a Friday treat. I love these shows!

Don't sweat the small stuff.
~Richard Carlson

Behavior Chart

My behavior chart was simple. Each child had a pocket envelope with their name on it. I taped the pocket envelopes in alphabetical order by first name on a poster board. The poster board was kept in full view of the classroom but behind my desk so that a child would not be tempted to change their color to a more desirable one. Yes, children can be sneaky and desperate.

The pocket held slips of colored cardstock in this order: green, yellow, red and blue. Every child started the day on green and hopefully stayed on green. Green meant *go*, yellow meant *slow down* and red meant *stop*. Blue was for a dreaded *trip to the office* for a "Come to Jesus" meeting with the principal or assistant principal along with a call or note home to their parent.

A consequence followed a child's card being put on red. A few minutes sitting on the bench during recess usually worked because it was embarrassing and frustrating. I always talked to children before releasing them to play with the other children. I wanted to make sure they understood what they had done to lose a privilege and to apologize if needed.

Teacher Tale: Shortly after the new school year began, I asked Briley, a neighborhood kindergartner, "Have you met my grandson, Brody? He is in your class."

"Ya, he got turned on yellow."

Later I asked Brody, "How was your day at school?"

"I got turned on yellow."

"What did you do?" I asked.

"I don't know," he answered.

Teacher Tip: Always send a note home if a child has been disciplined or hurt. If a child needs to see the school nurse, a note should go home from that office.

Increase Rewards as the Year Progresses

The color behavior chart worked fairly well the first semester of school. If necessary, I made the rewards more enticing as the year progressed. On each behavior pocket envelope, I paper clipped a sticker sheet. Children earned a sticker for every day they stayed on green. A child was allowed to pick something from the Treasure Chest when their sticker chart was full. It took twenty stickers to earn this reward. A well behaved student could earn something about once a month.

I pulled out the Treasure Chest on Friday afternoons only, wishing all that was needed for a reward was a smile or praise. Some years I did not use the Treasure Chest and I liked that better. It was time consuming and I had to buy the treasures or I asked parents for donations. But the children were proud of their sticker sheets and so were their parents. *Whatever works.*

Prevention

Preparing children in advance for a change from one activity or environment to another helps them manage the transition. With time, parents and teachers recognize a child's trouble spots. Then prevention can be accomplished before a problem escalates.

An ounce of prevention is worth a pound of cure.
~Benjamin Franklin

Dare to Discipline

Life is full of consequences. Natural consequences help children learn to take responsibility for their actions. Long-term gains offset short-term self-centeredness. It is essential for our society that we all learn to accept responsibility for our actions.

It is important to remind a child that it is the behavior that is disliked, but the child is still loved.

Remember you are the adult. Children forget, and forgive, faster than adults. You have to spend time with a child and explain that appropriate behavior has rewards. Inappropriate behavior has consequences. Be firm and do not give in once a consequence has been deemed necessary.

Ignore or Use Gentle Firmness

For some infractions, the simple act of ignoring the behavior will make it disappear. Repeatedly telling a child to stop doing something may make the behavior reoccur just for the attention. It is a sad fact that for some children, any attention is better than no attention.

Quiet facial clues may be all that is needed for a child to stop unwanted behavior. There are 43 muscles in the face. Children are good at figuring out animated facial clues such as frowning, pouting, sadness, or being afraid or horrified. My favorite is the Evil Eye Stare. I can stare down any five-year-old. Placing your hands on your hips seems to make the stare more powerful. It is comical to witness a child imitating this stance. And children will imitate adults.

Sometimes just putting your hand on a child's shoulder can signal them to stop unwanted behavior. Remember, you are the authority figure. They want your approval. They don't want to be embarrassed in front of their classmates, have you write a behavior note home, make a dreaded phone call to a tired stressed parent, or be sent to the office. I was amused at the surprised look on the kindergartners' faces when they learned I knew their parents' phone numbers.

Adults can often use their voices as tools for maintaining control and preventing many problems in the first place. Facial expressions and body movements can be used to emphasize words like, "Slow down." "Be careful." "Let's not get too crazy."

You need to move close to a troubled child, not yell from across the room. Sit or kneel close to the child and talk directly to them. Look kindly and intently into their eyes, perhaps taking gentle hold of their arms or shoulders. If you are upset, take deep breaths and remind yourself that you need to remain in control and be a good example of anger management.

Keep It Positive

Both parents and children get tired of hearing "no" all the time. Positive statements teach children what is appropriate. It is not enough to tell a child what not to do; you should also teach a better alternative. Explain why you cannot cater to the child's wishes. Give an explanation such as: "So no one gets hurt. So everyone can learn. So we can hear. Because it is good manners. So we can have friends. So everyone can have a turn. So everyone will have fun."

Give Choices

Even young children like to feel they have a choice rather than that they are being forced into something. Think carefully about the choices you offer before starting the negotiations. Give a choice and time when this wish may be available. Explain to the child why they may need to wait. It is all right to say, "I understand, but we must do school work before center time." Sympathize with them but set expectations with rewards. Even you, the leader of the classroom, have a boss who also has a boss. I found it amusing that the children were surprised that I had a boss, the principal. And the principal and I had lots of bosses, the parents. Mr. Key, a much beloved principal, once told me that I worked for the parents. They were paying my salary through property taxes. That comment helped me through several parent/teacher conferences.

Pick Your Battles

Some issues are not worth the hassle. You may feel as if you're giving in, but there are times when you should decide if what the child wants can be accommodated, at least at some time. Of course, you cannot run a free-for-all but goals and rewards are lucrative. It may be a better solution than a confrontation.

It is not all right for a child to be disruptive to the learning of other students. You may need to place the child away from the others until he/she is ready to join again in the learning process. Sometimes a little isolated time will bring a child back refreshed, and even humbled, and you've had a little break.

The harder the conflict, the more glorious the triumph. ~Thomas Paine

What Works

Ideally, a consequence should follow inappropriate behavior immediately. The consequence should be fair in relation to the behavior. Time out may be a good starting place. Be respectful. Adults need to be clear, firm and specific about what they mean. Don't resort to belittling a child. Some discussions need to be held in private. Unfortunately, in a school setting, a consequence may need to wait. Be sure the child remembers why they are sitting on the bench watching the other children play.

If an immediate consequence is needed, place the child in a corner facing the wall. Time out is honored for good reason. Time out teaches the child that for every action there is a reaction. Specifically, time out achieves two important objectives: it stops unwanted behavior and it offers a cooling off period for the child and for the adult.

The number of minutes the child is in time out should be equivalent to his age. Time out for a five year old should be five minutes. A discussion should follow so that the child knows why they received a time out and an assurance that a new start is certainly feasible. I often told the children, "You begin every day on green. It's up to you to make good choices today. You can do it. I'm here to help you. I want you to do your best."

What Does Not Work

You are the adult and role model. You are bigger than the child. Yelling and hitting are unacceptable and will only increase the child's yelling and aggressive behavior. Of course, this is never appropriate at school and hopefully not happening at home. Teachers are required to report suspicious signs of neglect or abuse to Child Protective Services. Teachers should also notify the school counselor and principal of concerns.

Aggression

A reason that spanking is not an effective form of discipline is that it can backfire. Imagine this: A five-year-old hits his four-year-old brother. The parent rushes in and hits the older child. What did the children learn from this scenario? They learned that it's okay to hit when they're mad, exactly the opposite of what the parent intended to teach. Children are masters of imitation and look to their parents as models.

Studies confirm that children who are treated aggressively will grow up to be aggressive. Thus, the potential is increased for the cycle of abuse to repeat itself through the generations. Do not hit children when you want them to stop hitting. Do not yell at children to tell them to stop yelling. Do not spit at children to indicate they should not spit. Of course, you want them to know how it feels, but you have to show them how to act, not how *not* to act.

When to Seek Help

Seek professional help if your child is doing dangerous or risky things that you can't stop, if he's overly aggressive with others, or is disrespectful of people, animals or property. Parents should also seek consultation if they notice unwanted changes in behavior or if there are physical signs such as headaches, poor eating or sleeping habits, or frequent bedwetting. Schools offer group and individual counseling. Ask for help, advice or a referral. Curing problems when a child is young will certainly make the teenage years better for everyone.

Maslow's Hierarchy of Needs

Psychologist Abraham Maslow first introduced his concept of a hierarchy of needs in his 1943 paper "A Theory of Human Motivation" and his subsequent book, *Motivation and Personality*. His theory is still taught and respected today. Simple needs must be filled in order to progress to the next step and before learning and self actualization can be accomplished. The lowest levels of the pyramid are made up of the most basic needs, while the more complex needs are located at the top of the pyramid.

1. Physiological Needs: The strongest needs are biological necessities for oxygen, food, water, and relatively constant body temperature.
2. Safety Needs: When all physiological needs are satisfied and are no longer controlling thoughts and behaviors, the needs for security can become active. Children often display signs of insecurity and the need to be safe. Separation anxiety is an example.
3. Needs of Love, Affection and Belonging: When the needs for safety and for physiological well-being are satisfied, the next class of needs for love, affection and belonging can emerge. People seek to overcome feelings of loneliness and alienation. This involves both giving and receiving love, affection and the sense of belonging.
4. Needs for Esteem: When the first three classes of needs are satisfied, the needs for esteem can become dominant. Humans have a need for a stable, firmly based, high level of self-respect and respect from others. When these needs are satisfied, the person feels self-confident and valuable as a person in the world. When these needs are frustrated, the person feels inferior, weak, helpless and worthless.
5. Needs for Self-Actualization: When all of the foregoing needs are satisfied, then and only then are the needs for self-actualization activated. This can be described as a person's need to be, and to do, that which they were "born to do" such as become a musician, artist, teacher, nurse, doctor, counselor.

Patience

One time a speaker at church ask that we turn off our phones and put them away. I had to nudge my husband who was reading on his phone. "Scriptures?" I asked.

"Uh, well, no, not actually." He was reading a cowboy novel. He put the phone away and we focused on the prepared talk.

Patience is the ability to put our desires on hold for a time. It is a rare virtue in our fast-paced world of instant messaging, game gratification and global news. People blog, tweet and surf the Internet more than they read books. However, more people are reading books now on their iPods, Kindles, Kobos, Ereaders and Nooks, which is encouraging.

Impatience is a symptom of selfishness or being self-absorbed. Children must learn to wait if they are going to reach their potential. They need to realize results don't appear automatically, but take time and effort.

Children, like adults, make mistakes. Children, like adults, want others to give them the benefit of doubt. Listen before you react or give a consequence, because once a consequence is given, it should not be reneged.

Dieter F. Uchtdorf writes, "Patience means staying with something until the end. It means delaying immediate gratification for future blessings. It means reining in anger and holding back the unkind word.... Patience is a process of perfection."

Be a Responsibility Role Model

Many Americans are remaining in a state of perpetual adolescence. By failing to move forward with grace and dignity, they are leaving a gaping hole in our fragile society. Many adults are treating relationships like disposable diapers, tossing marriages and children away because of selfishness. This displays a lack of responsibility and respect for others.

In some cases, it may be necessary to obtain a divorce due to abuse, but if all possible, counseling should be obtained before divorce with priorities focusing on the children. Make a commitment to stay together if possible. Love and marriage have various cycles. Respect encourages stability. It takes more giving than receiving when it comes to children (and often to spouses). Teachers must learn this early in order to last in this career.

> *Children need models rather than critics.* ~Joseph Joubert

Forgiveness

Children forgive easily and love unconditionally. It is amazing how short they hold a grudge. A simple sincere "I am sorry" works wonders. Adults should take lessons from them on forgiveness. When I made a mistake at school, I told the children, "I'm sorry. I was wrong." The look on their face was worth making that simple statement. They seemed to grow an inch taller.

Be a Team Player

Support your grade level team in every way possible. Meet once a week to plan and share lesson plans, ideas and materials. This will save you time and keep you on tract with the required essential elements. If you must leave your room, make sure someone covers for you. Never, ever, leave children unattended. This can put children in jeopardy as well as your career.

Support your principal and assistant principal and they will support you when you need it. And you *will* need it. Be kind to all the staff and they will help you. I was offered free cookies from the cafeteria workers on Fridays because I complimented them. The custodians brought me whatever I needed because I appreciated and respected them. The computer lab tech helped me teach the children about computers and programs when I lacked the skills. The office staff protected me from ungrateful parents. The principal, assistant principal and special education teachers supported me in Special Education meetings because I supported them, too.

Let It Go

Teachers are required to attend many workshops. I heard some teachers remark, "If I only learn one thing today that will help me, then it will be worth it." One day, I learned three powerful words that helped me numerous times: *Let It Go*. A teacher/author explained that it was all right to "let it go" rather than to win every argument, even if you are right.

One of the children's favorite weekly themes was the study of dinosaurs. Of course, the children always want to know why dinosaurs aren't around anymore to enjoy. I explained numerous times that no one really knows, but it might have been because of volcanoes, droughts or even a meteorite or comet.

Peyton, a freckled face, red-haired boy said, "It is because a giant volcano erupted and killed the dinosaurs. My dad told me so."

I answered, "That could be the reason. They could have died from an extreme change in temperature caused by erupting volcanoes, or perhaps a huge meteorite hit our planet."

But Peyton wouldn't give up. I saw the fire in his eyes as he defended his father's explanation of why these magnificent creatures no longer roamed our earth. Volcanoes were as exciting explanation as any. I certainly wouldn't want to insist that I knew more than Peyton's beloved father.

"Peyton, I'm sure your dad knows more than I do about dinosaurs." The look of pride in Peyton's eyes was worth more than my winning the uncertain.

Teacher Tip: Some teachers stopped doing the dinosaur theme because dinosaurs are extinct. But I spent a week on dinosaurs because children are fascinated by these huge creatures that once roamed our earth. Many math, science and reading activities can be implemented into this theme. I cut huge "dinosaur" feet out of cardboard and the children moved them around on the playground. It is fun for the children to make dinosaur fossils with sand and shells. Dinosaur Food is a huge hit also. See Chapter Nine for recipes.

Family Time

My friend Donna and her husband have been married 56 years. Donna said to Raymond, "I have some good news and I have some bad news, and they are both the same thing. We have each other." They made a commitment to marriage and they both have a wonderful sense of humor which pulls them along through the difficult times.

The following is quoted from Susan B. Carter's *Historical Statistics of the United Sates, Millennial Edition*: "In 1920 the divorce rate in the United States was 8 per 1,000 married women; by 1979, it had reached nearly 23, a nearly threefold increase."

It has dropped slightly, but this is likely due to a large increase in cohabitating couples, now an estimated 6.6 million (*American's Family and Living Arrangements: 2009*), whose separations, including from children, are not recorded in official statistics. By many measurements, the United States has the highest divorce rate in the world.

"Evidence of the toll is that today in America a heartbreaking 40 percent of all births are out of wedlock" according to Brady E. Hamilton, et al. in *National Vital Statistics Reports 58:16*.

Successful families require that men and women make substantial and long-term sacrifices of their time, money, and personal fulfillment in order to dedicate their efforts to rearing the next generation. ~Bruce D. Porter

Joke: Did you hear about the teacher who was helping one of her students put on his boots? He asked for help and she could see why. Even with her pulling and him pushing, the little boots still didn't want to go on. By the time they got the second boot on, she had worked up a sweat.

She almost cried when the little boy said, "Teacher, they're on the wrong feet." She looked, and sure enough, they were. It wasn't any easier pulling the boots off than it was putting them on. She managed to keep her cool as together; they worked to get the boots back on, this time on the correct feet.

He then announced, "These aren't my boots."

She bit her tongue, rather than get in his face and scream, *Why didn't you say so?* Once again, she struggled to help him pull the ill-fitting boots off his stinky little feet. No sooner had they gotten the boots off when he said, "They're my brother's boots. My mom made me wear 'em."

Now she didn't know if she should cry or laugh. But she mustered up what grace and courage she had left to wrestle the boots on his feet again.

Helping him into his coat, she asked, "Now, where are your mittens?"

He said, "I stuffed 'em in the toes of my boots."

She will be eligible for parole in three years.

The Perfect Kindergarten Parent

School counselors put helpful tips in the school newsletter. I would recommend the following in my classroom newsletter:

- Make sure your child eats a healthy breakfast.
- Put your child to bed by 8:00 p.m.
- Snuggle and read together every night possible.
- Turn off the television and do things together like puzzles, board games, drawing pictures,

exercising, riding bikes, playing outdoor games and communicating.
- Check your child's backpack for notes and homework. Read all notices sent home. Mark on your calendar special days such as school picture day, Grandparent's Day, holiday parties, and school performances.
- Attend Parent/Teacher Conferences.
- Telephone and leave a voicemail, or email teachers, with questions or concerns. Ask for a conference, or write a note, if you think your teacher needs additional information about your concerns or if there are changes at home affecting a child's behavior.
- Send an absence excuse when your child returns from missing school.

Children can feel if you love them or not. I survived as long as I put the children first. I had a mission: to teach academics and for the children to enjoy school, in other words, to have fun while learning. I couldn't do that if some of the students were misbehaving. I did truly love my students and my job. Sometimes I spoke it verbally and sometimes I used the sign for "I Love You." The children would sign back to me. They wanted me to succeed on some level. All children need and deserve love and this is the true test of teaching. If they feel that you have their best interests at heart, they will support you and love you unconditionally.

My daughter hears the words "I love you" every day. I'm lucky enough to hear the most precious words in the universe, "I love you, too." Tell children that you love them over and over again. This will build trust that they can come to you with any problem. Then be sure and listen without interrupting. If you don't know the answer, tell them, and search for answers together.

Chapter Seven
The Special Education Experience

Patience means accepting that which cannot be changed and facing it with courage, grace and faith. ~Dieter F. Uchtdorf

One year, I was hired to be a half-day special education teacher and a half-day kindergarten teacher. I had three severely autistic students in the morning who I taught one-on-one. They were extremely introverted and just wanted to *stem*. This is a term used for repetitive behavior, like flapping a book open and shut, or shuffling cards over and over.

My job was to teach them academics, draw them out of their inner world, and help them to stop stemming. University students visited my room to observe and offer me the latest research tips on how to teach autistic children.

Some days I felt frustrated and knew not much progress was occurring. The parents of one student put a lot of pressure on me to teach their son to read, although no one else had been able to accomplish this goal. Another student had mild to moderate seizures every day. And the third student was a severely mentally retarded student named Luke.

Luke lived in a Mental Health/Mental Retardation institution. His parents abandoned him. Every morning I met Luke as he got off the school bus. At first, he wanted nothing to do with me. His former teacher had to escort him to my room. But I soon discovered that Luke liked M&M's. I was not ashamed to reward him as often as I thought it needed to be done. Luke slowly responded to me. Eventually, he got off the bus, took my hand, and escorted me to the room.

This may seem like a small feat. But I was thrilled that he took my hand. Luke never learned to read but he got better putting puzzles together. He looked me in the eye more frequently. He stopped stemming so much.

The institution where Luke lived was closed in our town and he moved to another town. I still think of him and wonder if I had any impact. But then I remember he finally smiled at me and even got excited when he saw me. This might be a small thing to many, but it meant I had connected with a severally autistic child—an abandoned child.

Teacher Tip: It is all right to give a child M&M's if that helps the bonding process. Keep trying different things until you find the perfect reward. Ask parents, former teachers, and children what they like for rewards. Ideally, it doesn't cost any money and is time spent playing a special game or reading a certain book.

...had I listened to the voices in our culture telling me that I should spare myself the trouble and heartache of bringing a child with special needs into the world, our family would have missed out on the most positive and life-changing thing ever to happen for us. ~Sarah Palin

The Little Box of Cards

I was a substitute teacher and finally offered a job the second half of a school year. The former teacher of a kindergarten class was asked to not come back. She had difficulty managing the students. My daughter was attending this school and I was eager for a full-time position but wondered if I could manage a classroom that another teacher could not.

Enrolled in this class was a student who suffered from depression. He cried for no normal reason. I tried to encourage him into the world of learning. Nothing seemed to work. I begged his mother to take him to a doctor after she admitted he had been diagnosed as bipolar. She said she could not afford the medicine. I listened to his low pitiful moan daily. I had twenty other children I was responsible to teach. Some days I had to ignore him. It was painful for everyone.

It was a long semester. I was spending most of my conference time trying to help Ben who refused to go to Special Areas. Mr. Key, the principal, offered to let him sit by his office if I had work to do, or needed a break. *No kidding.* Finally, the nurse convinced Ben's mother to take him to a doctor.

Ben improved slowly. He quit crying every day. Eventually, he listened in class and even responded to questions. The other children started playing with him. We all helped pull him out of his huge hole of depression.

Toward the end of the school year, Ben's mother told me she was going to move and they would be living in another school district. I encouraged her to leave Ben in our school until the school year was over. This child had too many adjustments in his short life and he wasn't coping well. Mr. Key agreed that he would let the child stay because the year would be over soon.

On the last day of school, Ben brought me a small gift box. I had many gifts that day, bigger and in prettier bags with lovely cards. But I liked Ben's gift the best. Inside were tiny note cards. I can't write much on the card but I only use them for special occasions. I won't ever use my last card because I don't want to lose the memory of that precious child and his generous gift. We were all better for having him in our school. He pushed our limits and we rose to the occasion.

Children are like that, small precious gifts. We teachers only have them for a brief time, but they can impact our lives, and the lives of other students, in a gigantic way.

Was I successful with this child? I'd like to think that I helped build his self-esteem, make friends, and enjoy life more. I can't truthfully say that I brought him to a higher level of academics. But he finally talked to me, smiled, and even gave me a hug. He began to laugh and play with other children. That was my reward. I looked for Ben the following year but never saw him again.

Teacher Tip: Always be friendly with the school nurse. She will help you through difficult times. She cares about children or she would not be working in an elementary school. She will send sick children home who are spreading germs

If you have concerns about physical, mental, or emotional concerns about a student's wellbeing, ask the nurse, counselor, assistant principal or principal to help you. That is their job. They have more training and more pay. Maybe a parent volunteer or an aide has a little extra time to help with a time-consuming child. Thirty minutes of help can go a long way when you have a desperate situation.

Alice, a friend of mine, did not realize that she could be a school volunteer, even when I teaching. And I did not know that she wanted to help, but didn't know she could—a simple lack of communication. Schools require minor paperwork before one can volunteer including a criminal background check. Now Alice volunteers in a kinder classroom once a week. She helps with a literacy group and enjoys it very much. I'm sure the teacher greatly appreciates her help with this group of struggling readers. Alice told me her favorite student gave her a Christmas present. It was a broken black crayon wrapped in wrinkled paper with a few lines scribbled on it. She smiles when she talks about the little boy's gift.

All the world is full of suffering. It is also full of overcoming.... I long to accomplish a great and noble task; but it is my chief duty to accomplish small tasks as if they were great and noble. ~Helen Keller

Tucker spells T-r-o-u-b-l-e

Oh my, did I have a challenging class one year of teaching. Boys outnumbered girls three to one. This was definitely not fair. Ask any kindergarten teacher.

Tucker's mother was unmarried and pregnant with her second child and she was only eighteen. She and Tucker lived at her grandparent's house. One day, a little boy told me that Tucker had shown his "pee pee." At first, I did not believe it. This had never happened to me before, even in kindergarten. Tucker vehemently denied the accusation. I did not witness it, so I gave him the benefit of doubt. Surely, he had not done such a thing with little girls in the room who would undoubtedly tell their mommies.

But it happened again and Tucker vehemently denied it again. After more questioning, Tucker admitted the truth. I took him to the office.

The principal called Tucker's mother and reported the reasons her son was sitting in her office. When school was over, Tucker's pregnant mother and her tattooed, body-pierced boyfriend appeared at my classroom door. She started screaming at me that I was a liar, and that I picked on her child, who had never done anything wrong in his entire life. This was after numerous behavior notes were sent home by all the special area teachers, as well as myself. She also insisted that he was gifted even though testing did not confirm it and I should do something about it. *Like what?*

I called the counselor and asked if we could all come to her office. The principal joined us. It was not a fun hour as I was accused of many things, of which teaching Tucker to read was not even mentioned.

I was hurt, discouraged and angry. Why should I have to spend so much time on a disrespectful, annoying, hyper little boy, his unappreciative mother, and her scary-looking boyfriend? I was feeling grossly underpaid. Once again, my principal supported me.

A few weeks later, Tucker was taken to the office by a cafeteria worker. She had witnessed Tucker showing his private parts underneath the table. Tucker's humbled mother was summoned by the principal to a meeting. He was suspended for three days. *Thank you.*

I was somewhat elated that I had a three day break from Tucker and would have a break from his mother and her scary boyfriend as well. When Tucker returned to school, he brought me a note. It said, "I am sorry that I lied. You are the best teacher ever. I love you."

I knew I must forgive this five year old child. I hugged him and told him that I loved him too. I promised Tucker he could be the Super Star next week if he had good behavior. After all, he was the only one left who had not been a Super Star and he wanted it badly.

He earned it. I never saw such a happy Super Star. He led the line as he held my hand. He helped me with errands like taking papers to the office (escorted by a mature kindergartner who had never been in any trouble). He was even visited by the principal and complimented for being such a great student.

One day Tucker said, "I went to my little sister's shower. And she wasn't even there!" She was still in the womb. I sent home an inexpensive baby gift.

On the day of our Christmas party I received a beautifully wrapped present from Tucker. It was two wine glasses with little candles. They looked like they came from the dollar store. But they were the pride of my collection of candles. I had earned them.

Tucker's mother told me on the last day of school that Tucker loved me and that she had been wrong in not believing me. She told me I was a great teacher. She had heard I was going to retire and hoped Tucker was not the reason. I assured her that he was not the reason but that I needed to be at home with my special needs' daughter. I wished her the best and we hugged as a few tears rolled down my cheeks. There's a lot to be learned, and earned, from forgiving others.

Teacher Tip: Document. Document. Document. Years later, I learned that this child was classified as Emotionally Disturbed and in an alternative classroom. The special education process had taken several years.

Some schools do not test children in kindergarten for special education hoping the children will "mature" out of their inappropriate behavior. Some children come to school already having a label as they were diagnosed early and attended early childhood special education classes.

It is difficult for a teacher to be patient when she knows something is wrong with a child. Be persistent in asking for help and to have the child tested. Keep a record of events that show inappropriate behavior or significant delayed learning. Inform the principal and diagnostician of your concerns. Never give a parent a diagnosis. This is for a qualified diagnostician or psychologist to do after thorough testing.

Do not have any part of the room inaccessible to your eyes. Have eyes in the back of your head, or at least be able to turn your neck like an owl. Never leave children unsupervised for any length of time.

Parent Tip: If you have concerns that your child is developing at a slower rate than normal, or has "issues", or delayed speech, please obtain help in the early years. Government or school testing and services are available and free from birth. Call your local school for a referral or ask a pediatrician. The earlier that problems are diagnosed, the better prepared you and your child will be for school.

Joke: A kindergartner asked his teacher, "What is it called when somebody sleeps on top of somebody?"

The teacher's face reddens as she answers, "Jesse, I think you'd better ask your parents that question."

The next day, Jesse came back to school and promptly told the teacher, "It's called bunk beds."

Autism

Brody, my kindergarten grandson, talked to me after their dog had been run over by a car.

"One time my dog died. My dad got a shobel and dug a big hole. We had a fun'ral and put a cross on his grave."

I was sad with him, yet I am delighted to hear any words Brody speaks. He was diagnosed as autistic when he was three but has made remarkable progress. His parents think the progress was due to tubes being put in his ears after numerous ear infections, chiropractic adjustments (neck perhaps out of alignment during birthing), therapeutic horseback riding lessons, and early childhood intervention programs which included speech, physical and occupational therapy.

One doctor told Brody's mother that sensory/motor/integration problems are sometimes misdiagnosed as autism. Brody's language was delayed and he flapped his hands and walked on his toes. Those symptoms have disappeared. He is now classified as having Pervasive Developmental Disorder—Not Otherwise Specified (PDD-NOS) which is still on the spectrum of autism but with not as noticeable characteristics. As with any child, structure, preparation, routine and consistency help, especially when combined with therapies.

I wonder how often autism is misdiagnosed, as is Attention Deficit Hyperactivity Disorder (ADHD). Do we give children drugs for their benefit, or for our benefit?

Every child is a blessing, a gift waiting to unfold. ~Larry Davis

Tips for Admission, Dismissal and Review Meetings (ARDs)

There are federal mandates and state legislation regarding Special Education. Parents, and teachers, should be aware of Special Education students' rights. Testing is required before a person qualifies for services. Services are available from birth, and throughout one's life, if qualified.

A certified diagnostician or psychologist is qualified to test for educational purposes. After extensive testing, a child qualifying for special education services must have an Admission, Dismissal and Review (ARD) meeting to discuss the student's Individualized Education Program (IEP). In the state of Texas, the ARD committee meets at least twice yearly to discuss, amend and approve the document. Special education students are tested every three years and may be tested more often if it is requested by a parent or teacher. Special education students are to be in a regular education classroom for as much time as determined it will still be enhancing them academically. This is called *inclusion*. A *Resource Room* is a special education classroom taught by a certified special education teacher usually with several aides assisting so that small group, or one-on-one instruction, can be offered.

The longest ARD meeting I attended lasted four hours. It was exhausting. The staff held a meeting beforehand so that agreement was reached among us as to what was best for this child. We determined that the autistic student's needs would be best met if he spent some time in a resource room the following year. His kindergarten year had been full inclusion or spent entirely in a regular education setting with an aid. The diagnostician's proposal was that it was in the child's best interest for him to receive special education teaching in the resource room for one hour a day.

The parent did not want her child to spend any time in a special education classroom. Thus, the four-hour meeting slowly progressed. She was a member of a parent's support group for autistic children who strongly advocated for full inclusion. We finally convinced her that it was in his best academic interest for him to spend 45 minutes per day in the resource room and this period would include his travel time to the resource room and back. She finally, but reluctantly, agreed to the school's recommendations.

Teacher Tip: Teachers should always have a brief meeting with the diagnostician and principal (or assistant principal) before an ARD so there are no surprises. Always support the staff in a meeting. Be prepared to tell positive accomplishments about the child as well as concerns and goals. Be respectful and positive.

Teacher's Toolbox: Faith, hope, and charity.

Parent Tip: Take your spouse, a grandparent or a friend with you to ARDs. You will need their support. I attended my child's first ARD with no support. I felt alone and overwhelmed with the school staff which included a diagnostician, speech therapist, occupational therapist, physical therapist, assistant principal and teachers. I needed the offered box of tissues. Be prepared and make a list of things you would like discussed and any information which would be helpful for the staff. Be on time and respectful. Everyone has your child's best interests at heart.

Principal Tip: Be open to having special needs' people volunteer in your school. Perhaps they can Xerox, prepare mailers, monitor in the cafeteria, or play a game with a child who needs extra attention. My daughter was allowed to volunteer on Friday afternoons in my kindergarten room. She read books to children, colored examples, helped children learn the alphabet, played board games, picked up centers including finishing puzzles, and helped during recess time. She was a friend to a shy or introverted child.

I will always be grateful to my principal, Mrs. Staniszewski, for allowing my special needs' daughter to volunteer in my kindergarten classroom. Sarah still talks about it with fond memories. Now Sarah and I serve in the church nursery and she continues helping children who love her unconditionally. This is a win-win situation. She also has a business called Sarah Farms. She has chickens and sells fresh farm eggs. This teaches her responsibility and monetary value.

A Personal Note

As a mother of a special needs' daughter, I've often asked myself *Why? Why me? Why her?*

I'm past that now. I left the guilt feelings behind and just enjoy my daughter and the wonderful times we have together. I tell other people, "If it weren't for Sarah, I wouldn't be at the zoo today, or swinging at the park, or riding the train for the umpteenth time." Sometimes people look at us a little strangely, but I feel like the blessed one. I love swimming, animals, and nature and have the perfect excuse to venture outdoors. It appears that my daughter will be "forever young" as her brother Ian likes to say. Her sister Kim agrees and said, "Growing up isn't all that it's cut out to be."

Special needs' people have sweet spirits full of love. It is a fun and rewarding job being the parent of a person who sees or experiences life differently from "normal" people. They are here to teach us compassion, patience, how to be in the moment, and to enjoy the simpler things in life.

First I was told what he could not be, then I learned what he was not, and now I understand his potential and how much my interaction plays a part in his future. ~A Parent's Perspective

Chapter Eight
Silly Sanity Lists

What Should You Teach Children?
The 10 Rs
>Reading
'Riting
'Rithmitic
Restore
Reuse
Replenish
Recycle
Responsibility
Respect
Role Model

What Can You Learn from Children?
The 10 L's
Look—the first word you can read—then do it
Listen—to children and to senior citizens
Love—conquers all
Linger—on spiritual writings for support, insight and survival
Learn—everyday try something new
Live—each day to the fullest
Laugh—give a big smile to someone every day. They'll smile back.
Lemonade—make lemonade out of lemons (this may refer to adults too)
Ladybugs—are fascinating, friendly and fun to hold—but are they all ladies?

Lollipops—come in many kinds and colors, just like people.

> *What sunshine is to flowers, smiles are to humanity.* ~Joseph Addison

The Survival Cs

Collaboration—Teachers must let go of their egos and work together as a grade level team. Always support your principal and all staff. Then they will support you when you need it. And you will need it.

Cooperation—Children can learn the meaning of this word. Everyone benefits.

Creatures—Children love classroom pets. Let them name and help care for them. Animals have tender souls and promote healing. Teach children kindness and respect for all creatures.

Celebration—Life is a celebration. Use the word *celebration* instead of *party*. It produces less of an adrenaline rush with children.

Care—Tell the children that you care about them. That is why you have rules. So everybody can learn and no one gets hurts. Criticize the behavior, not the child.

Concern—Be concerned. Report unusual behavior, neglect or abuse to your school counselor. Reporting to Child Protective Services may be required. Ask the school counselor for individual or group counseling for a child who needs it. Inform families of community services when needed.

Creativity—Hands-on learning is the best teaching tool. Go to garage sales and buy craft supplies, an electric skillet (see Chapter Nine), books, games and a wagon for hauling.

Consistency—at school and at home. Put your classroom schedule in your newsletter. Advise parents to be consistent and have a schedule at home. Inform parents of upcoming events. People don't take change well. In other words, keep everyone informed with no big surprises. Children like having a behavior or a chore chart at home. Everyone loves to check off accomplishments on a list. It's really fun with a red pen which seems to create a sense of power or make a child feel like a teacher.

Church—Church offers support at many levels. Children learn morals, manners and social skills as well as learning that a Heavenly Father loves them. Church attendance can save parents time and money instead of taking them to a psychologist later when they struggle through the teen years.

Choose—Always choose the right thing to do.

Children—We are all children of a Heavenly Father. Be childlike: forgiving, spontaneous, adventurous.

> *Never think you have been taught enough.* ~Henry B. Eyring

The Parent/Teacher Conference

Don't Criticize
Don't Compare
Don't Complain

Begin the conference by telling the parents something positive about their precious child. Be prepared. With parents of disruptive children, tell the parents in your most caring manner, looking them in the eye, that you are concerned about their child's behavior. You only want what is best for their child, after all. Be a good listener and you will gain insight as to why problems are occurring. This insight may give you that extra bit of patience to deal with the child's behavior.

You may want to ask for permission to have a child tested by the school counselor for play therapy. Parent's permission is necessary but I never had a parent decline. This gave me thirty minutes once or twice a week of classroom time to concentrate on other children. And it gave the counseled children some special attention, pampering and an outlet for their frustration.

Inevitably, someday you will have a special needs' child in your classroom who has not, as yet, been diagnosed with any disorders. Gently talk to the parents about your concerns. Never give your personal diagnosis. Sometimes parents already have a feeling that something is wrong and are relieved when a teacher suggests testing. Some parents are offended and in denial. Thus, testing by a profession clarifies if a child qualifies for special education services.

The Four Ps for When You Need a Substitute

Plan: Always leave well-written plans and prepared paperwork. You never know when you may become ill or an emergency happens in your family. Make sure your lesson plans are clearly displayed on your desk along with the required paperwork.

Prepare: "Always Be Prepared" should be every teacher's motto. Large groups of children do not function well with unstructured time. Leave extra work and books for the substitute. Make sure she/he knows the children have a journal for writing and drawing during any down time. The children should also have a school library book in their desk or cubby. Our school librarian's policy was that library books were not to be taken home in kindergarten. I understood this because sometimes the books were lost or damaged. Look at garage and library sales to build your classroom library. Many people having sales will donate their unsold books to your classroom rather than haul them somewhere else.

Play Dough: I never met a kindergartner yet who doesn't love play dough. See Chapter Nine for recipes.

Pray: The best advice I ever received regarding a parent/teacher conference was given to me by my friend Lynn. She is a retired Special Education District Supervisor. She told me that she would say a prayer while walking down the hallway to meet with an upset parent.

Be Thrifty—Look for Garage Sale Goodies

I'm like a magnet being sped toward a sale. Freebies are even better. My parents grew up during the depression and *Frugal* was their middle name. I guess I inherited that trait. I've heard my husband say about me, "Give her something old, a can of spray paint and she'll have something useful in no time." Here are some helpful teaching items that can be bought inexpensively at garage sales:

- Craft supplies
- Wagon
- Electric skillet for making play dough, Apple Crisp and no-bake cookies
- Crock pot
- Popcorn air popper
- Ice trays
- Yarn, string and rope. The rope is for a Texas, or a cowboy theme (not to be used as a disciplinary tool). Children love to jump rope. Teach them rhymes as two children learn to swing the rope for another child to jump through. This is easier said than done. I usually hold one end of the rope. Children love Tug of War. Have them wear gloves to protect their hands. Place two children on flat stones or behind tape and tell them to stay there while they tug.
- Mixing bowls

- Holiday decorations
- Children's Books (remember Golden Books are needed at the Christmas book exchange)
- Games
- Puzzles
- School supplies
- Scissors
- Glue gun and glue sticks
- Sidewalk chalk
- Flower vases. You can put fresh flowers in the vases during your Mother's Day Pampering Party. Reasonable re-gifting is all right if you are a teacher. I always gave parents who volunteered a small gift at the end of the year with a note of gratitude. It is the thought that counts. A few chocolate brownies or even a chocolate candy bar shows gratitude. I don't know anybody who doesn't like chocolate. If you can't afford that, a Thank You note is underrated and will be cherished.

Keep your craft supplies after you retire. Much to my surprise, I was asked to be a Cub Scout Den Mother after I "retired". Now I serve in the nursery at church. Children love crafts.

Myth: Teachers get a three-month break during the summer.
Fact: Teachers often work summer jobs in order to pay back student loans. Many teachers attend summer workshops to become better teachers.

Myth: Teachers make too much money.
Fact: Teachers are allocated a small amount of money for their classroom supplies. Math manipulatives, wooden puzzles, education games, and large books are expensive. Teachers spend personal

money for necessary supplies and desirable teaching materials.

Teacher Tale: June, my retired teacher friend, shared this story with me from her first year of teaching.
"Having been financially pinched while going to college, I drove an ancient Volkswagen Beetle which often failed to start. I would park at the top of the school parking lot which sloped downward. Then after the long day, I could push the car from the parking space, head it down the slope, running beside it to jump in and pop the clutch. Voila! It would start.
"One day, Jimmy raised his hand after the Pledge of Allegiance and asked, 'May I ask you a question?'
"I, of course, replied, 'Yes.'
"He asked, 'Why do you chase your car down the parking lot?'"

Priceless Gifts

Gifts don't need to be costly to be appreciated. Some of my favorite gifts have been:

- Pictures of me drawn by students showing me in a variety of poses and doing amazing acrobatics with "I Love You" written on them.
- Christmas ornaments, including hand-made ones. I treasure them each year when we decorate our tree.
- Thank you notes written by parents.
- Hugs from former students after they run across the playground to see me.
- Parents who compliment me to the principal.
- Parents who apologize for their child's behavior and promise to support me in discipline.
- Supportive spouse who has dinner ready when I come home and protects me for fifteen minutes

from anyone asking me any question. I couldn't give an intelligible answer anyway, especially by Friday evening. I could only answer in one syllable words or a head shake.
- A photo album of events that had taken place that year.
- A book with pictures drawn by my students. This was a secret collaboration by homeroom moms and the art teacher. Mrs. Jaramillo helped my 2003-2004 class illustrate the book. Below are the words underneath the pictures. I received a beautiful hardbound copy. But I would have also cherished a 3-hole punched notebook. It was the thought, effort and time that were greatly appreciated. Below are the words for each letter in case a room parent would like to make a book for their child's teacher, should that teacher be so fortunate.

The ABCs of Mrs. Case

A is for Appreciate! We appreciate everything you do!

B is for Beautiful: Mrs. Case is the Most Beautiful Teacher

C is for Caring: Thank you for caring for us.

D is for Determined: You are determined to be the best teacher you can be.

E is for Extraordinary: You are an extraordinary teacher.

F is for Fun: You make learning fun.

G is for Great: You are the Greatest!

H is for Happy: You make us happy.

I is for Ideas: You have the best ideas.

J is for Joy: It is a joy to have you as our teacher

K is for Kind: You are very kind to us.

L is for Love: We love you.

M is for Magnificent: You are magnificent.

N is for Nice: It is nice to be in your class.

O is for only: You only have our best interest at heart.

P is for Patient: Thanks for your patience with us.

Q is for Queen: You are the queen of our class.

R is for ready: You make us ready to learn.

S is for sad: We are sad you will not be our teacher next year.

T is for Terrific Teacher: You are a terrific teacher.

U is for unbeatable: Mrs. Case, you are unbeatable.

V is for Very: You are the very best teacher.

W is for Wonderful: You are wonderful.

X is for X-ray: If you x-rayed your heart, you would find a big smile.

Y is for Yell: You never yell at us.

Z is for Zip-pa-di-do-da: Zip-pa-di-day We love you!

Lists and Calendars

Children and adults benefit from making lists. When you write something down on a piece of paper it serves as a reminder. Now your brain doesn't have to keep remembering it. Relevant dates are posted in the school and classroom webs and newsletters. Keep a schedule of daily events in your classroom and also in your newsletter to inform parents and visitors. The class may be outside for recess or in special areas. The schedule gives parents and children a sense of security, stability and preparedness. Parents and children benefit from keeping a family calendar.

Eleven Uses of Crayons

I have witnessed children using crayons in the following ways:

1. Tear paper off crayons
2. Stick pencil into crayons breaking pencil tip
3. Glue crayons together
4. Break crayons by pressing them down on desk
5. Chew on crayons
6. Stick crayons up nose and into ears
7. Cut crayons with scissors
8. Color desk with crayons and try to erase with pencil eraser before the teacher notices
9. Carefully place crayons in rows sometimes sorting by size or color
10. Run hands over and over rows of crayons for sensory-motor integration
11. Finally the goal is reached—print their name!

We could learn a lot from crayons; some are sharp, some are pretty, some are dull while others bright, some have weird names, but they have all learned to live together in the same box. ~Robert Fulghum

Chapter Nine
Recipes for Fun Fridays

Part of the secret of success in life is to eat what you like and let the food fight it out inside. ~Mark Twain

Need a break from constant questions, chattering and whining? Fun Fridays is your answer. Children cannot talk, or at least cannot be understood, with food in their mouths. This is especially true if they are missing front teeth.

Here are some ideas to go along with teaching a letter of the week. Include a *Desired Supplies List* in your newsletter so parents can contribute, or even make, a treat. It is all right, and necessary, to have parent contributions. Yes, I realize some schools do not allow sweets to be given to children except on rare occasions. When at all possible, give the children fresh fruits, vegetables and whole grains. It would be impossible to make all of these recipes in one year. These are ideas to supplement the letter of the week when the children deserve a treat, or when you want to emphasize a letter. I've also included some of my favorite recipes that you could make for special occasions such as the Mother's Day Breakfast.

You may be surprised how many children have never tasted some of the foods offered to them. Upon a dare, most children will try the green eggs and ham and even love them. **Be sure you are aware of any food allergies, such as nuts, glutton, or dairy**.

Apples—Read books about Johnny Appleseed. Ask each child to bring one or two apples. Chart the apples by color: red, green and yellow. Count and pattern apples. Let the children peel the apples with an apple peeler slicer corer which produces a very long peel. It has a clamp to attached to a table. The children love to turn the wheel and watch with pride and amazement as a very long peel is accomplished. Ask the children to put their peels in a row according to length. The following recipe smells delicious and can be cooked in an electric skillet.

Apple Crisp (already tripled for a classroom)
1 1/2 cups quick-cooking rolled oats
1 ½ cups packed brown sugar
3/4 cup flour
1 ½ teaspoons cinnamon
3/4 cup butter
6 pounds apples (about 15)
6 tablespoons sugar

Melt butter in electric skillet. Add oats, brown sugar, flour, cinnamon and a dash of salt. Peel, core and slice fruit to make approximately 15 cups. Mix with other ingredients. Cover and stir occasionally. Save some for the principal and custodian because the heavenly aroma will float down the hall.

Bananas are inexpensive and nutritious. Slice down the middle and fill with peanut butter. Cut into pieces and freeze. The children will love having something frozen in their mouth.

Banana Splits
Ask parents to contribute and let children make their own banana split. Offer toppings of Marchino cherries, whipped topping, nuts, M&M's, chocolate and caramel sauce.

Blackberry Surprise Muffins
4 cups all-purpose flour
3 cups sugar
1 1/2 cups shortening
4 teaspoons baking powder
2 cups milk
2 teaspoons salt
2 teaspoons vanilla extract
3 cups fresh blackberries
pinch cinnamon
1 cup chopped pecans or walnuts (optional)

Preheat oven to 375°. Blend together flour, sugar and shortening. Mix in baking powder, milk, salt and vanilla and fill muffin pans half full. Place a blackberry in the center of muffin. Spoon on some of the reserved mixture covering the blackberry. Bake in 375° oven for 18 minutes. Makes 24 muffins.

Banana Bread
Cream:
1 cup sugar
1 cup butter, softened

Add and beat well:
2 cups flour
½ teaspoon soda
1 teaspoon baking powder
¼ teaspoon salt

Add to dry ingredients to make a creamed mixture:
½ cup buttermilk (or regular milk)
1 cup mashed bananas (2 large ones)
½ to 1 cup chopped pecans (optional)

Mix until well blended. Pour into greased and floured bread pans. Bake in 350° oven for 1 hour and ten minutes. Makes two loafs.

Bread, Pumpkin
3 1/2 cups flour
1/2 teaspoon baking powder
2 teaspoons soda
1 1/2 teaspoons salt
1 teaspoon cinnamon
1/2 teaspoon cloves
pinch of nutmeg
2 2/3 cups sugar
2/3 cups vegetable oil
4 eggs
1 16-oz. can pumpkin
2/3 cups water
1 cup chopped pecans (optional)
½ cup raisins or chocolate chips

Combine dry ingredients. Add wet ingredients. Bake 350° for 35-40 minutes in greased and floured pans. Yield: 4 medium loaves or makes 24 muffins. The bread will be very moist if you let it sit for 2 to 3 days. This bread freezes well.

Bread, Strawberry
3 cups sifted flour
1 teaspoon soda
1 teaspoon salt
1 teaspoon cinnamon
2 cups sugar
4 eggs, beaten
1 ¼ cup oil
2 (10 oz) packages frozen strawberries, thawed using juice

Optional
1 ¼ cup chopped pecans
pinch of nutmeg
1 mashed banana

Sift flour, soda, salt, cinnamon and sugar into large bowl. Combine eggs, oil, strawberries and pecans. Make a well in the center of dry ingredients. Add liquids, stirring just enough to moisten. Pour into two greased 9x5x3" bread pans. Bake 350° for one hour. Or use 6x6x3" pans to make six small loafs. Remove from oven and let stand five minutes before removing from pans. This bread becomes moister if allowed to sit a few days. The bread freezes well and makes pretty Christmas loafs because of the color from the strawberries..

Carrots, cantaloupe and cucumbers. The children will be surprised to learn that pickles are made from cucumbers. It takes time to roll and cut dough for shaped cookies, a tradition that seems to be diminishing from our society. The children will greatly appreciate the effort.

Cookies, Christmas—Francina Dulin (my mother's favorite)
1 pound butter, softened
2 ½ cups sugar
3 eggs well beaten
1 tablespoon white Karo syrup
5 cups shifted flour
1 teaspoon baking soda
1 teaspoon chopped pecans (optional)
2 teaspoons vanilla

Cream butter; add sugar and vanilla and cream thoroughly. Beat eggs well. Add Karo to eggs and add to first mixture. Sift flour with soda and add. Mix in nuts. Roll into rolls and wrap in waxed paper. Refrigerate. Roll out and cut with cookie cutters dipped in flour. Sprinkle with colored sugars or with a sugar and cinnamon mixture. Pecan halves are especially good baked in the center. Bake on lightly greased, or ungreased, cookie sheets in 350° oven for 8 minutes. Makes 12 dozen cookies if dough is cut to 1/8 inch thickness.

Cookies, Sugar
½ cup butter, softened
1 cup sugar
1 egg
1 ¾ cups flour
1 teaspoon baking powder
1 tablespoon milk
½ teaspoon vanilla
¼ teaspoon salt

Preheat oven to 375°. Cream butter and sugar, then add egg and mix. Add remaining ingredients and mix until smooth. Refrigerate dough for two hours. Roll out dough 1/8 inch thick on lightly floured surface. Dip cutters into flour before each use. Place on ungreased cookie sheet. Bake 12-15 minutes or until lightly browned. Place on cooling rack for 5 minutes, remove from sheet and cool. Makes 24-30 cookies. You may need to double this recipe as it can be difficult to roll dough thin enough.

Cookies, Sugar Free Oatmeal
1 cup whole wheat flour (or use half white)
1 cup oatmeal, Quick-cook
1 teaspoon cinnamon
1 teaspoon baking powder
½ teaspoon baking soda
¼ teaspoon ground nutmeg
¼ teaspoon ground allspice
¼ teaspoon ground cloves (optional)
½ cup raisins
1 cup unsweetened applesauce
¼ cup water
1/3 cup vegetable oil

2 eggs
1 teaspoon vanilla extract
¼ cup finely chopped nuts (optional)

Combine all ingredients in a mixing bowl. Beat well. Drop by spoonfuls onto a lightly oiled baking sheet. Bake in a 375° oven for 10-15 minutes or until browned. Makes 48 cookies.

Cookies, Gingerbread
This recipe can also be used to make ghost cookies with a little reshaping of the dough. Preheat oven to 375°. In a large bowl, sift and mix together:

3 cups flour
¼ teaspoon salt
1 teaspoon baking soda
1 teaspoon ginger
1 teaspoon cinnamon
¼ teaspoon ground cloves
¼ teaspoon ground nutmeg

In another bowl or mixer cream:
12 tablespoons (1 ½ sticks) unsalted butter, softened
¾ cup brown sugar
1 egg

Stir dry ingredients into the creamed mixture and add:
½ cup molasses
1 tablespoon vanilla

Let dough rest at least 2 hours, roll dough ¼ inch thick and cut with gingerbread cutter. Bake 7 to 10 minutes on a greased cookie sheet. Do not peek! Makes two dozen cookies.

Chocolate Chewies Make a brownie mix and pour into a lightly greased pan. Pat chocolate chips and chopped pecans on top. Don't cook the full time and they will be chewier. Chocolate brownies are greatly appreciated by teachers for their birthday.

Chocolate in a Cup for Teacher Pampering

This is a one-person microwave cupcake for a tired teacher treat. It is quick and extremely delicious when eaten warm. Perhaps you'll need a scoop of ice cream.

4 tablespoons all purpose flour
4 tablespoons sugar
2 tablespoons cocoa
1 egg
3 tablespoons milk
3 tablespoons cooking oil
3 tablespoons chocolate chips (optional)
Splash of vanilla
1 large coffee mug

Add dry ingredients in mug, mix well. Add the egg, mix thoroughly. Pour in the milk and oil, mix well. Add vanilla and chocolate chips. Mix again. Put the mug in the microwave and cook 3 minutes at 1000 watts. The cake will rise over the mug but don't be alarmed. Allow to cool and turn out onto a plate. Let it sit awhile in your mouth for full flavor.

Dirt Pudding

1 (14 oz) bag Oreo cookies
2 (3 ½ ounce) packages vanilla instant pudding
3 cups milk
1 cup powdered sugar
1 (8ounce) package cream cheese, softened
¼ cup butter, softened
1 (12 ounce) container cool whip
Gummy worms

Break up cookies and put half on the bottom of a clean clay flower pot or child's sand bucket. Save other half for topping. Mix pudding and milk together, set aside. Mix sugar, cream cheese and butter. Add sugar mixture to pudding. Fold in cool whip. Pour onto cookies. Top with remaining cookies (or make more layers). Poke gummy worms into mixture. Refrigerate for at least a half hour when possible. Serve with gardening trowel or a child's plastic shovel.

Dinosaur Food (Chocolate Oatmeal No-Bake Cookies)
½ cup dirt (cocoa)
½ cup swamp water (milk)
2 cups crushed bones (sugar)
½ cup fat (1 stick of butter, softened)
3 cups grass (uncooked Quick-cook oatmeal)
½ cup squashed bugs (peanut butter, optional)

Mix dirt and swamp water. Add crushed bones and fat. Heat to boil for a full minute in electric skillet. Add grass. Remove from heat. Add bugs. Cool and place on waxed paper by spoonful.

Eggs. Read Dr. Seuss' book *Green Eggs and Ham*. Cook chunks of ham and scrambled eggs in an electric skillet. Use a few drops of blue and yellow food coloring to produce green eggs. If you don't want to use food coloring, perhaps you can find green shelled eggs laid by Araucana chickens to show the children. The color of these eggs range from pale turquoise to pale olive green and the eggs taste great. Let the children use water colors, Q-Tips, and paper plates to combine the primary colors of red, blue and yellow discovering how different colors are made.

Fruit Loops can be used for patterning, making necklaces and to glue on paper forming first names. Ask parents to send fresh fruit and combine for a fruit plate.

Fossil Dough (enough for 24—not edible)
2 cups salt
6 cups flour
2 cups cold brewed coffee
2 cups used coffee grounds
1 cups sand

Mix the ingredients in a large bowl. Knead the dough until smooth then store in an airtight container. Have students collect a variety of leaves, shells, twigs, feathers and small plastic insects or dinosaur. Give each child a portion of dough and encourage students to roll it into a ball and then flatten slightly. Have them press an object evenly into the dough. Gently remove so its impression is left behind. Allow fossils to air dry for approximately two or three days. Turn the fossils over after one day so that both sides will dry.

Fruit Ring with 7 up Drink
Lightly spray oil inside of a bunt pan. Put in fruit such as from a frozen mixed fruit package. Or use fruit chunks of strawberries, blueberries, mango and Marchino cherries. (Bananas may brown). Add pink lemonade or cranberry juice for a pink color. Leave room in pan for freezing because liquids expand when frozen. You may need to set the pan in hot water to thaw the ring enough to loosen it. Place frozen ring in punch bowl and add more 7-up or pink lemonade. This makes a beautiful and interesting drink which I used for my Mother's Day Breakfast.

Fudge, Delicious and Non-Cook

2 lbs. powdered sugar
1/8 teaspoon salt
1 tablespoon vanilla
1 cup chopped pecans (optional)
1 (8 oz) package cream cheese, softened
½ lb. butter
½ cup cocoa

Melt butter; add cheese and stir. Add remaining ingredients and mix well. Makes 2 rolls on foil. Refrigerate then slice to serve. Looks festive with Marchino cherry halves.

Fudge, Super Easy can be made in the classroom if you have a microwave or electric skillet.

14 oz. can sweetened condensed milk
12 oz. package semi-sweet chocolate chips
½ cup chopped pecans (optional)
1 teaspoon vanilla extract

Microwave milk and chips in a bowl on high 1 to 1 ½ minutes. Stir until smooth. Add vanilla and nuts. Coat bottom of pan with oil or it will stick. Spread into 9-inch pan. Cool and cut in squares.

Grapes may not be available for some children to eat due to the cost. I was surprised and humbled at how appreciative some of my students were to have grapes. Seedless is recommended. Gummy worms could be a treat to place in front of a well behaved student. Quickly the other students will behave to earn their worm.

Goo is not edible but fun to touch. Have children sit in a circle. Mix cornstarch, water and food coloring in a bowl on a plastic tablecloth. Pass the bowl around for the children to touch. Do not this mixture leave unsupervised in a center although the children will beg you to let them play with it some more.

Honey. Read books on bees. Make honey sandwiches or eat honeydew melons.

Haystacks
Melt a bag of Butterscotch chips. Nestles, rather than the store brand, works best. Microwave on high for 1 ½ minutes. Add 10 oz. of Chinese Noodles and place in piles on a sheet of wax paper.

Ice Cream—Add a can of frozen grape juice to a gallon of vanilla ice cream for purple cow ice cream. Then have children draw and color a purple cow. Read a book about children living in a different culture. Does the color of our skin, hair or eyes matter? Not to kindergartners.

> *I never saw a Purple Cow,*
> *I never hope to see one.*
> *But I can tell you, anyhow,*
> *I'd rather see than be one.*
> ~Gelett Burgess

Jelly Beans. Have children count, sort and pattern before eating. Put some in a small glass jar and ask children to predict, or estimate, the number before counting together. Make Jell-O Jigglers. The recipe is on boxes of purple and orange Jell-O around Halloween.

Kisses. Have parents send various kinds of Hershey's Kisses. Children can match and pattern before eating. Kiwi is a delicious fruit that few children have experienced.

Lollipops, lemon drops, licorice. Make lemonade. Watch their faces pucker. Lemon cheesecake made with yogurt is healthy especially when using sugar-free gelatin. Or just make some lemon pudding. The children can help.

Lemon Cheesecake
2 graham cracker crusts
2 packages sugar-free lemon gelatin
1 1/3 cup boiling water
2 packages light cream cheese, softened
2 cups flavored lemon yogurt (or add a few drops of lemon concentrate to plain or vanilla yogurt)
1 12 oz. container of whipped topping

Pour gelatin into blender; add hot water and blend. If you have a food processor, just use hot tap water. Add cream cheese and blend again until smooth. Pour into a large bowl. Lightly stir in whipped topping. Pour into piecrusts. Marchino cherry halves make a pretty garnish. Let chill at least 4 hours before serving. I sprinkle pecan pieces over mine for adult parties.

M&M's make good sorting and counting math manipulatives. Of course, they will end up in the more immature children's mouths quicker than those who try and follow directions.

Marshmallow Limbo. Tie marshmallows on a piece of dental floss then hang them from a long string tied across the room. Play music and let the children limbo underneath catching a marshmallow in their mouths. Serve hot chocolate with marshmallows. An electric tea pot, crock pot, or microwave in your classroom is beneficial.

Noodles, Nerds candy, Neapolitan ice cream, nachos.

Oranges, Oreo or oatmeal cookies. Put different kinds of onions in jars or baggies so the children can smell them. Did you know some cows are called "oreo" cows? They are black on the ends and have a white middle stripe. I have also seen "oreo" pigs which are pink on the ends and have a white center stripes.

Peanut Butter sandwiches cut into shapes using cookie cutters or cut to make triangles or squares. The book *Peanut Butter and Jelly: A Play Rhyme* by Nadine Bernard Westcott can be ordered on Amazon.com. You can listen to the lyrics on this site:
www.songsforteaching.com/jackhartmann/peanutbutterjelly

Pigs in Mud
Miniature pink marshmallows in chocolate pudding.

Pig Slop
Combine chocolate pudding with M&M's, raisins, coconut, cereal, candy, chopped apples and bananas.

Play Dough
The children will enjoy watching you make play dough especially as you add the food coloring or perhaps a few students could add a few drops. Use your electric skillet and a wooden spoon.

2 cups flour
1 cup salt
2 cups water
2 tablespoons cooking oil
4 teaspoons cream of tartar

Mix and heat until ingredients form a ball. Add a touch of food coloring or scent such as peppermint, orange extract or vanilla. Or add texture such as glitter or oatmeal. Store in a covered container or closed baggie.

Play Dough—No Cook
2 cups self-rising flour
2 tablespoons alum (in spice section)
2 tablespoons salt
2 tablespoons cooking oil
1 ¼ cups boiling water
Add a touch of food coloring and scent if desired. Mix, knead, and store in a covered container.

Punch—Slushy
2 cups sugar
1 (6 oz) package of strawberry or cherry Jell-O (for pink color)
6 cups hot water
2 (46 oz) cans pineapple juice
4 (1 qt) bottles ginger ale

Mix sugar and Jell-O. Add hot water. Stir until dissolved. Add pineapple juice. Pour in plastic containers. Freeze at least 24 hours. Remove from freezer about 1 hour (or more) before serving. Add bottles of cold ginger ale. Mix to slushy consistency.

Popcorn popping out of an air popper is fascinating to kindergartners. Colored popcorn can be found in specialty stores during the Thanksgiving season. The colored corn makes beautiful decorations. Draw a small ear of corn on paper with kernels. Have the children place one colored kernel on each section. This is a good project for fine motor skills.

Teach the "Popcorn Popping" song by Georgia W. Bello. You can google to find a You Tube video as well as the book to purchase on Amazon.com.

Quaker Quick Oats—show children the word *Quaker* and *Quick* on an oatmeal box. Collect containers from parents and make drums for rhythmic patterns. See oatmeal cookie recipe under C.

Rasins. Rings are inside of Cherrios, Fruit Loops and donuts. Cut strips of red, yellow and blue paper. Have the children glue the rings together in patterns of red, yellow and blue. Staple all the children's rings together for a long chained pattern to string around the room. Children love to make wagon wheel pasta necklaces. Dye the pasta using food coloring and a tiny amount of vinegar in baggies. Spread wheels on newspaper to dry. Children can make these into patterned necklaces and wear during the Thanksgiving Feast.

Salty, Sweet and Sour. Have the children taste a salty cracker, sour pickle, sweet candy and a bitter olive.

Shaving Cream is a fun treat to rid the desks of crayon marks and germs. I saved this for a Friday "bribe." Unscented is probably best in case a child has allergies.

Sprouts are interesting to watch grow, nutricious and inexpensive. I have the best luck sprouting lentels. You only need ¼ cup for a quart of sprouts. Wash beans then put in quart jar and fill with water. Cover jar with cheese cloth or some material. Leave overnight in a dark place. The next day, rinse beans and do not add more water. Each day, the beans will sprout a little more. It is not necessary to put in a dark place and this can lead to forgetfulness. Out of sight—out of mind. There are many helpful You Tube videos on the Internet to watch before you sprout. The children may enjoy watching one as well.

Tweety Bird Treats. Have parents contribute to a trail mix: Cherrios, raisins, nuts, sunflower seeds and M&M's. Use your electric skillet to make Tortilla Triangles. Put a little grease in electric skillet, place several tortillas on bottom, top with cheeses, place another tortilla on top and turn over to cook on both sides. Cut into triangle shapes.

Upside Down Pineapple Cake
1 box yellow cake mix
1 cup brown sugar
3 eggs
1 stick butter
1 can pineapple (rings or chunks)
1 ½ cups liquid from pineapple juice and water

This cake can be made in an electric skillet. Mix 3 eggs in with the cake mix in a bowl. Add pineapple and water juice mix. Melt butter in skillet. Reduce heat to low. Sprinkle 1 cup brown sugar over the butter. Place pineapple on top of brown sugar. Spoon cake mix over top of pineapple. Cover skillet and let cook on low heat for about 20-25 minutes or until mixture has the consistency of cake. Let cool, turn upside down and cake will fall out.

Volcano—In small supervised groups, let the children add baking soda with vinegar into a mound of clay to make an "explosion".

Volcano Cake
Spray a 9x13 pan with Pam. Sprinkle 1 cup of chopped pecans and 1 small bag of coconut in bottom of pan. Mix up a German Chocolate cake mix according to box directions. Beat in a mixer for greater volume. Pour over the nuts and coconut. Beat together 1 stick of soft butter, 1 box of powdered sugar and one 8 oz. softened cream cheese. Again, beat in mixer for greater volume. Heat this mixture 1 minute in the microwave for easy pouring. Pour on top of the German Chocolate cake mixture. Poke holes with a toothpick in the topping so that it will not burn. Put the 9x13 pan on a cookie sheet because there may be spillage. Bake in 350° oven (325 for glass pan) for 55 minutes. Cool before serving.

Watermelon, Wheat and Water. Study how water turns into ice and vapor. Let the children pour water into ice trays and put a few drops of different food coloring for a variety of colored ice cubes. Later take the ice cubes out while the children observe them melting and changing states again.

X—Make letters out of Pretzels. Review straight letters before children eat the pretzels. There are fifteen stick figure letters (A, E, F, H, I, K, L, M, N, T, V, W, X, Y, Z). Children could form their name with pretzels and licorice before eating.

Yogurt, or yellow cupcakes with yellow icing. Put a yam in some water and it will slowly root and grow leaves.

Zebra stripped cupcakes. Arrange twenty-four cupcakes into a zebra shape. Use chocolate and vanilla icing to make stripes.

There are only two food groups. One—foods that you cover with cheese. Two—foods that you cover with chocolate. ~Author Unknown

Chapter Ten
It's a Wonderful World, After All

In today's crazy rushed world, we hear too many negative stories. I have seen people go above and beyond what is required. We witness heroes everyday performing deeds of kindness, expecting no reward. I know many heroes and so do you.

> *It is our light, not our darkness, that most frightens us. We ask ourselves, Who am I to be brilliant, gorgeous, talented, fabulous? Actually, who are you not to be?* ~Marianne Williamson

Random Acts of Kindness

I went to the convenience store counter to pay for some drinks. The cashier told me, "Somebody already paid for those."

I asked, "Do I look that desperate?" We had just come from the zoo on a very hot day. I had gulped down some of my drink and refilled it before putting on the lid.

She laughed and said, "No, ma'am. Sometimes this happens."

Earlier that day, I'd given a conductor's hat to our local zoo for the train ride. I didn't need it anymore since I retired from kindergarten. The grateful conductor insisted on giving my daughter and me a free train ride. That same afternoon a stranger bought us drinks.

Join the Random Act of Kindness Day on February 17th. Make a Difference Day is October 23rd when many Americans graciously give of themselves and their time to help others. World Kindness Day is November 13th.

Do something spontaneously, or anonymously, for somebody. Any day will work.

Some free things that have a positive effect on our world are to vote, share, smile and pray. Learn to be more grateful, humble, courteous, complimentary, positive and helpful. It doesn't cost money to leave a person, or place, in better condition. When you do make purchases, buy American made to create jobs.

> *Look for opportunities and they will present themselves.* ~John Locke

Teachers are Heroes

A friend of mine, June, was Teacher-of-the-Year twice in her school district. She helped her fifth graders make quilts during the study of the westward expansion. It took weeks of painstaking stitches. They are cherished. She also encouraged her students to come to school early and taught them how to crochet. It surprised her how many boys came. Don, an active boy, excelled by making a vest in a Granny Square design that he proudly wore to school. This activity gave some children a place to be instead of waiting outside in the cold and something fun to do after finishing their work before class ended. June is retired now but helps organize a book club, volunteers for Meals-on-Wheels and helps with church activities.

Mrs. Johnson, an elementary music teacher, has inspired her choirs to win numerous state championships. She was been honored with too many awards to mention here. What I remember about Mrs. Johnson is that she encouraged a boy in a wheelchair to participate in the choir. At first, Mrs. Johnson pushed his wheelchair, helping him get onto the bus for trips. Later, children pushed the boy's wheelchair. The choir won many trophies for being the best in singing but I know they also portrayed the best in character building.

Elementary School Principal Mrs. Stanziwinski strives to know every student by name. She greets the handicapped children as they come off the bus and encourages them to have a wonderful day. Superintendent Dr. Braswell attends every function and activity possible, presenting numerous awards to deserving teachers and students.

I know community leaders who support schools with grants for books, science supplies, benches, raffle gifts and whatever else a school may need.

I know teachers who have donated money to feed the hungry. They have bought shoes, coats, backpacks and school supplies for their students when the parents did not have the money. Teachers donate whatever they can when a catastrophe occurs including fires and flooding of students' homes. Many teachers stay after school tutoring without pay, and without much appreciation. They do this because it is the right thing to do.

I've worked in schools where blood drives are held for students, their family members, or for staff. Fundraisers are often accomplished through a group effort of schools and communities.

After I retired, I mailed a box of favorite children's books to an army chaplain. Soldiers are videotaped reading a book to send home to their children.

Recently, I initiated a service project for our church members to donate school supplies for the Operation Iraqi Children project. I was helped by many volunteers.

Thankfully, I know teachers and principals who will never take the "God" out of the Pledge of Allegiance. Daily, my principal, or a student, leads the pledge proudly over the loud speaker. Many schools in our state follow with the Pledge of Allegiance to the Texas state flag, which newcomers to our state find curious. The pledge is "Honor the Texas flag; I pledge allegiance to thee, Texas, one state under God, one and indivisible." Our school was also blessed to have a Minute of Quiet Time every day for everyone to meditate, pray, or think positive thoughts. This started our day with a positive attitude.

> *My success was not planned but it could only happen in America.* ~John Grisham

Adults are Heroes

A pessimist sees a glass as half empty, an optimist sees it as half full, a volunteer asks, "Who needs a drink?" I have church member friends who help children tie blankets for the Salvation Army and for a children's institution. Bolts of material have been donated by a local clothing manufacturer. My special needs' daughter has earned money to buy material and ties numerous blankets which she donates. Special Needs' people should be encouraged to do service. Sarah and Jennifer work in their church nursery. Kim sews pillows, Krystle works at a daycare center, Molly works at an office, and Stephanie volunteers at her former high school.

I know a parent who gave a generous gift card to a family when the mother had twins which inspired other parents to contribute. I know parents who spend countless hours volunteering for schools helping with fundraisers, office work, teacher projects, crossing guard, tutoring, cafeteria monitor and anything else requested. My niece, Denise, was awarded the PTA Life Membership Award for her numerous hours of volunteering.

I know parents who spend time with their children, who together struggle with homework, who praise their children often and punish them when they deserve a consequence for a wrong choice. Bob, a pilot, made an extra flight home to view the last twenty minutes of his daughter's ballerina recital. He said it was worth the extra flight home to be there for her.

I know parents who have accepted, and grown to love, a disabled student in their child's classroom. These are the same parents who complained to the principal at the first of the year when an autistic child was having difficulty adjusting. I know parents who notice when a child is neglected and offer to help the struggling parent or grandparent who is raising the child.

I know a mom who offered to take care of a student so that his mother could switch to a day shift and spend more time with her sickly child, also enabling the child to spend less time in a daycare. I know a mom who takes care of a friend's children early in the morning, feeds them breakfast, and drives them to school so that their single mother can arrive at work on time. I know mothers who babysit children free of charge after school so that single mothers can work. I know Home Room Moms and even friends of teachers who make sure the teacher and children have whatever supplies are needed.

I know women who donate or alter dresses for girls to wear to the prom. Hairdressers fix their hair for free. The girls are pampered with free manicures and makeup for their special night. I know women who sew baby bereavement gowns to donate to hospitals or who crochet premie caps for the Neonatal Intensive Care Unit.

Mark's cowboy church had an auction to benefit the youth foundation. Mark bid highest on a teenage bullrider named Ty. The boy was interested in the horses and mules that Mark trained. He was supposed to work a week but worked the entire summer helping Mark around the ranch. This gave Ty not only a good role model in Mark, but it also gave him a productive place to be. Ty's mother was free to go to work and not worry about her son spending too much time alone or unsupervised.

My friends have bought extra school supplies for my students. They brought me meals, chocolate, and foot pampering supplies when a little attention for a tired teacher worked wonders. I have friends who collect money and walk in the Relay for Life donating money to cancer research. Such friends pray for, and help boost, fellow teachers when they have cancer. Many teachers offer their sick days when teachers have no more and need chemotherapy.

I know men who have married single mothers with special needs' children and have adopted the child to raise and love as their own. I know husbands who cook dinner and take the children to after school activities so that the mother can go back to school and earn a degree. I know mothers who have forsaken their high-paying careers in order to be available for their children, putting families first.

It's times like these when the kindness of strangers —a compassionate doctor, an inspiring mentor, an unshakable advocate—can mean so much. It can mean the difference between hope and despair; sometimes even life and death.
~Kristen Russell Dobson

We all know police officers who put their lives on the line every day. They visit schools to talk about their careers, staying clean from drugs, and obeying the law. Jeff, an FBI agent, risks his life everyday trying to rid the streets of drug dealers. This agent jumped out of his truck when my daughter crashed her bike. He was genuinely concerned and helpful. (He also helped me move an antique couch I found by someone's curb when I didn't want to wake my husband and have him help me haul yet another freebie home.)

I know firefighters who bring their fire trucks to school, answer countless questions and let children explore the truck. These role models encourage others to make the right choices due to their strong moral fiber and good example. I know people who *volunteer* to fight fires, help in hospitals, and deliver meals to the sick or elderly.

My friend, Dr. McDaniel, researches seizure disorders and helps my daughter free of charge with treatment not covered on her insurance. I know dentists who donated numerous toothbrushes and toothpaste for Katrina hygiene packs. I know doctors who donate their time and talents to help people in dire medical conditions with no monetary compensation.

I know people who have adopted children from other countries and given them the opportunity to become whatever they dream. I know foster parents who have taken children or adults into their homes because they needed a home.

Charles Fletcher donated his ranch to offer special needs' people therapeutic riding lessons. One such student was adopted from Russia and had no arms. She learned to ride a horse by herself with the help of a hard vest with Velcro straps and the encouragement of angelic teachers.

John Katz and Gloria Saxon started a bowling league for homeschoolers. John is a retired police officer and veteran. Gloria worked for years with special needs' people and knew many homeschoolers have disorders and delays. This bowling league boosts children's self-esteem as well as activity level.

John's wife, Cindy, showed me a picture of her granddaughter who has cerebral palsy. She was surrounded with stuffed bunnies which she had gathered for Scottish Rite Hospital to be given to children at Easter time. She also collects bears and other stuffed animals so that every child can have one for Christmas.

I know people who have gone on missions with no pay except the reward of knowing that they helped others. Our church offers help all over the world often being among the first to respond to emergencies and catastrophes. Churches offer a kaleidoscope of opportunities for service.

Senior citizens take on roles of adoptive grandparents. Our daughter cherishes the crocheted blanket given to her by our neighbors, Johnnie Mae and C.D. They are genuinely concerned with her health and happiness.

I asked my teacher friend Larue about her father's philosophy on life. Lawrence George Kearl lived to be over 100 years old. Some of his favorite quotes were:

For as he thinketh in his heart,
so is he. ~Proverbs 23:7

I am only one,
But still I am one.
I cannot do everything,
But still I can do something;
And because I cannot do everything;
I will not refuse to do the something that I can do.
~Jeanie Ashley Bates Greenough

... choose you this day whom ye will serve ...
but as for me and my house we will
serve the Lord. ~Joshua 24:15.

My parents grew up during the Great Depression and sacrificed and saved for their five children's future. They tried to instill moral fiber into our backbones. Eventually, it paid off as we matured. My sister, Diane, volunteers in the local Emergency Room, the Salvation Army Angel Giving Tree and Meals on Wheels. My brother, John, volunteers to work in a vacation bible school. John took his saws and helped cut down trees after Hurricane Katrina. My brother, Mark, helps neighbors with carpentry skills or attends to their needs due to severe weather. My sister, Shryl, helps support her grandchildren with time and purchases. She also helps the elderly or ill in her neighborhood.

If you are a teacher, or a parent, you perform countless selfless acts of kindness every day. Pamper yourself.

I know good people. God answers prayers through people, through you and through me. I hope I can always be on the Lord's errand. I hope I have enough sense to accept help from others when I need it. They need to be a vessel of gifts too.

> *The best way to find yourself is to lose yourself in service to others.* ~Ghandi

Children are Heroes

Savannah, my granddaughter, told me her teacher asked children to bring shoeboxes to school. The children brought their gently used toys to donate as gifts. The boxes were carefully wrapped. Some precious toys went to children whose parents could not afford gifts at Christmas.

I know children who have donated all their money to feed hungry people. I know children who have pulled wagons around their neighborhoods asking for food donations for the community food bank. I know children who have donated their beanie babies and stuffed animals to soldiers to give a child in a war ravished country. Our grandson, Gavin, loves to help us with yard and garden work and helped my husband build a chicken house. We appreciate positive outlets for his abundant energy.

These scouts achieved the rank of Eagle Scout: John raised 1,000 pounds of food which was donated to the local food bank; Austin raised the money and volunteers to install lights at a free therapeutic horseback riding center; and Caleb raised money and volunteers to upgrade a park.

I know a twin who could have finished a long-distance race first, but stopped to help her sister when she fell. I know children who have pushed children in wheelchairs so that they could participate in Field Day relays. During Field Days, many principals, assistant principals, PE teachers and parents sweat outside all day in the Texas heat so they can cheer children to finish races.

One Sunday, during primary class, sweet Cydney told my husband, "You smell like eggs."

My husband replied, "I had bacon and eggs for breakfast this morning." *I must need to take my jacket to the cleaners.*

Cydney's mother later told my husband, "That was a compliment. Cydney likes eggs."

Cydney had her leg amputated below the knee due to a disease which affected bone growth. I watched friends push her around in a wheelchair during the healing process. Now they hold her hand as she wears her new leg and a big smile.

> *I always tell my kids if you lay down, people will step over you. But if you keep scrambling, if you keep going, someone will always, always, give you a hand. Always. But you gotta keep dancing, you gotta keep your feet moving.* ~ Morgan Freeman

Conclusion

I hope you have found something useful in this book. I now know that teaching was my greatest opportunity for service, sacrifice, and reward.

> *Our children are the promise of the future,*
> *Our hope for a better tomorrow.*
> ~National Black Child Development Institute

About the Author

Susan Case is a retired Special Education and kindergarten teacher and the mother of a special needs daughter. She earned a Master of Science degree in Family and Child Development and has teaching certificates in Early Childhood, Special Education and Elementary Education.

Visit Susan's blog at kindergartenbasics.blogspot.com

www.ingramcontent.com/pod-product-compliance
Lightning Source LLC
Chambersburg PA
CBHW061657040426
42446CB00010B/1774